Church Planting in the
AFRICAN AMERICAN COMMUNITY

Church Planting in the
AFRICAN AMERICAN COMMUNITY

Michael J. Cox
Joe Samuel Ratliff

Judson Press
Valley Forge

Church Planting in the African American Community

© 2002 by Judson Press, Valley Forge, PA 19482-0851
All rights reserved.

No part of this publication may be reproduced, stored in a retrieval system, or transmitted in any form or by any means, electronic, mechanical, photocopying, recording, or otherwise, without the prior permission of the copyright owner, except for brief quotations included in a review of the book.

Judson Press has made every effort to trace the ownership of all quotes. In the event of a question arising from the use of a quote, we regret any error made and will be pleased to make the necessary correction in future printings and editions of this book.

Bible quotations in this volume are from The Holy Bible, King James Version (KJV) and from the New American Standard Bible (NASB), © 1960, 1962, 1963, 1968, 1971, 1972, 1973, 1975, 1977 by The Lockman Foundation. Used by permission.

Library of Congress Cataloging-in-Publication Data

Cox, Michael J., 1957–
  Church planting in the African American community / Michael J. Cox and Joe Sameul Ratliff.
    p. cm.
  Includes bibliographical references.
  ISBN 0-8170-1401-2 (pbk. : alk. paper)
  1. Afro-Americans—Missions. 2. Church development, New—Baptists. 3. Southern Baptist Convention—Missions. 4. Southern Baptist Convention—Membership. 5. Afro-American Baptists. I. Ratliff, Joe S., 1950- II. Title.
  BV2783 .R35 2002
  254'.1'08996073— dc21   2001044713

Printed in the U.S.A.

08 07 06 05 04 03 02

10 9 8 7 6 5 4 3 2 1

CONTENTS

- vii **Foreword** by Charles L. Chaney
- xi **Acknowledgments**
- 1 Chapter 1
  Surveying Jesus' Journey and Our Journey
- 21 Chapter 2
  Learning from Those Who Have Gone Before
- 43 Chapter 3
  Sharpening a Vision for Church Planting
- 54 Chapter 4
  Understanding the Role of the Sponsoring Church
- 75 Chapter 5
  Understanding the Role of the New Church Pastor
- 89 Chapter 6
  Steering a Course through the Obstacles
- 109 **Bibliography**
- 111 **About the Authors**

FOREWORD

TWENTY-FIVE YEARS AGO I BEGAN TO THINK SERIOUSLY about the issues and problems related to starting churches in America's predominantly black communities. When I talked about that interest, my friends, both black and white, said, "No new churches are needed in black communities. Sometimes there are three storefront Missionary Baptist churches in one city block in the inner city!"

Their observation about the number and proximity of black churches is, of course, correct. And there is more. Large, strategic, and powerful black churches have been developed in the cities and suburbs of our nation. They have fantastic moral and political clout, and most of them are also deeply involved in evangelizing the lost and meeting social needs. These churches have been the prime movers in confronting drug traffic, providing housing, doing job training, and helping with employment. The institutional churches of the early 1900s have continued and expanded to form the great body of black churches operating today.

These facts stimulated a question in my mind: How did we get all these black churches in the inner cities of our nation?

My research uncovered what I believe is the greatest untold church-planting story of the twentieth century. In 1900 there were a few black churches in northern industrial cities; today there are thousands. This growth has mainly taken place without planning, outside support, or human supervision. It was done at great sacrifice by church planter-pastors who made their living apart from their church work. Their achievements have been enormous, and their legacy continues as new black communities develop and as established black communities change. What we have today is essentially the result of spontaneous church planting.

However, that paradigm is now shifting. Church planting in black communities has become more intentional. Under the Holy Spirit's leadership, strong black churches are deliberately training and sending out church planters. Pastors of predominantly black churches are supervising these church planters. Monetary support is coming from these sponsoring churches.

This book is the first serious effort to get at the nuts and bolts of this process. It is written by two men with experience in intentional church planting.

Foreword

Joe Ratliff is a genuine scholar-pastor with the heart of an evangelist. His church—Brentwood Baptist Church of Houston, Texas—welcomes thousands to Sunday worship and has an intensive, intentional commitment to multiplying new congregations.

Michael Cox has served as minister of youth in Joe Ratliff's church. Further, he has planted a strong church on the new paradigm and has been part of a national denominational team involved in church extension in predominantly black communities. He has been a leader in a national program for strategic planning for the megacities of North America. He now is the leader of the national program for church planting for the American Baptist Churches in the U.S.A. He is a young man marked for leadership in this arena as the new millennium gets under way.

Who should read this book?

- Everyone interested in church growth, church planting, and evangelism
- Everyone interested in reaching the great cities of America
- Leaders of denominational programs committed to church extension or new church development
- Leaders of predominantly black churches
- Leaders of churches in transitional communities
- Missions professors
- Seminarians
- All who love the Lord Jesus Christ and want to see the lost found

Foreword

- Those who care about impacting the moral culture of this nation with Judeo-Christian values
- Especially those who believe God is calling them to plant a church in a predominately black community

Although written primarily from a Baptist perspective, this book can be translated into any denominational language. I highly recommend it.

Charles L. Chaney
Research Professor of Missions
Southwestern Baptist Theological Seminary
Fort Worth, Texas

ACKNOWLEDGMENTS

THE AUTHORS WISH TO EXPRESS OUR LOVE AND appreciation to Michael's son and Joe's godson, Michael Phillip Cox; to Joe's loving wife, Doris Gardner Ratliff; to Michael's family, Mr. and Mrs. Thurman Cox Jr., Deborah Crayton, and Nathan Cox; and to Brentwood Baptist Church in Houston, Texas. They have continued to provide encouragement and inspiration in our journey to start churches in black communities across the nation.

We also want to express our appreciation to Dr. Aidsand Wright-Riggins III, Dr. David Laubach, Dr. Tom Van Johnson, Megen Verlenden, Margaret Dempsey, Russann Hadding, Vernastine Davis, and Rev. Charles Kerry Smith for their commitment to church starting in black communities and for their encouragement and guidance in the publication of this book.

CHAPTER 1

Surveying Jesus' Journey and Our Journey

LET'S EMBARK ON A JOURNEY. THIS JOURNEY WILL NOT be like a restful vacation at a mountaintop resort. Nor will it be a Sunday afternoon drive down an idyllic country road. Rather, it will be a difficult journey—one with curves in the road before us and turbulence in the sky overhead. And it will be a long journey, so that, once we have started, we may often wonder, *When are we ever going to get there?*

We may be tempted to ask, "Why should we make this journey, if it is so arduous and seemingly unending?" We make this journey because it is *necessary*. It is one of those trips that we know we must make, although, if given a choice, we might prefer not to go. Though difficult, this necessary journey is rewarding, and Jesus is our model as we start on our way.

JESUS' NECESSARY JOURNEY

In John 4 we read the familiar story of Jesus and his encounter with the Samaritan woman. In interpreting this passage we often focus on the relationship that developed between Jesus and the woman rather than on the journey that brought Jesus there. But this time let's consider the journey.[1]

John described the journey as necessary for Jesus, commenting, "He must needs go through Samaria" (v. 4, KJV). Although the most direct path from Judea to Galilee lay through Samaria, most devout Jews did not take this way. Because of the hatred and contempt that the Jews held for the Samaritans, they went out of their way to avoid them, even if such avoidance entailed inconvenience. But Jesus had no choice. Because of how the Father wanted to use him in the lives of some people—one in particular—it was spiritually necessary for him to take the direct path, to go through rather than around Samaria.

This necessary journey for Jesus was rife with difficulties.

First, the journey was *historically unprecedented*. The Jews had established a tradition of going around Samaria. Jesus shocked the religious establishment by ignoring history. He chose to make some history of his own.

Second, the journey was *culturally unacceptable*. The Jews saw the mixed-race Samaritan culture as an abomination of what God intended for the Jews to be. The cultural distinctives of the Samaritans were offensive to the Jews.

Third, the journey was *theologically unsound.* The Jews—God's chosen ones—were completely intolerant of Samaritans. The Jews had religious reasons to back them up. Surely God would agree with them (they assumed) in their idea that, because the Samaritans had corrupted their racial purity and had turned to pagan influences, they deserved no contact with God's elect. Rightfully, they were to be ignored and forgotten as much as possible.

Fourth, the journey was *politically inexpedient.* In Jesus' day political leadership and religious leadership were so intertwined that to offend one was to offend the other. Jesus risked offending not only the religious leaders but also the political authorities with his journey.

Fifth, the journey was *economically unfeasible.* Jesus relied on the generosity and goodness of others to meet his basic needs. Here, he was entering into enemy territory. He would not be welcome. He might not be cared for. He certainly would not be indulged. More than likely he would leave that place with nothing more than what he went into it with, possibly with less.

Sixth, the journey was *socially unacceptable.* Crossing through Samaria meant that, somewhere along the journey, the Jewish traveler would have to come into contact with the hated Samaritans. The Jews could think of no group of people whom they abhorred more than the Samaritans. The thought of having any social contact with the Samaritans was repulsive to the Jews.

Against these odds—historical, cultural, theological, political, economic, social—and perhaps others, Jesus set out on his journey. Despite the difficulties, Jesus accomplished what he set out to do. He was able to share the riches of his Father with one who was despised by others.

Was Jesus trying to make some kind of statement with his journey? We believe so. His statement is that the gospel is for all, not just for the elect, the rich, the beautiful, the white, the pure, the lovable ... The list could go on interminably.

The point of Jesus' necessary journey is clear: the gospel is for all people, in all the world.

OUR NECESSARY JOURNEY

Unlike Jesus' journey, our journey is not one that leads us through a certain territory. Rather, it is a "journey" of obedience to God in the starting of churches in black communities that will honor God and serve the needs of people. Yet it is just as necessary for us as Jesus' trip through Samaria was for him.

Church Planting in the SBC and ABC

Let's consider our journey primarily within the context of two denominations: the Southern Baptist Convention (the SBC) and the American Baptist Churches in the U.S.A. (the ABC). After watching the SBC develop an intentional strategy for church planting in the African American community since about 1989, we now see the ABC attempting to plant a significant number of churches in all communities.

The differences between the two denominations are enormous. As the ABC has led the way in fighting for the justice issues that are a significant part of any gospel message, it has lost some of its evangelistic fervor. And as for the SBC, while it has often ignored or responded too late to the social ills of our world, its Bold Mission Thrust represented an unprecedented denominational commitment to spreading the Good News.

The paths that the two denominations have embarked upon since their split over slavery and other issues in the nineteenth century have paralleled the approaches to racial reconciliation and healing taken by the country's two leading political parties. Like the Democratic Party, the ABC has taken a more activist approach to racial matters; meanwhile, like the Republican Party, the SBC has been more hands-off. Yet just as both political parties have largely failed at resolving the complex issues of race in our country, so the denominations' responses to African Americans and church planting have often led to harmful policies and attitudes in both communities, black and white.

Since publication of the first edition of this book in 1993, one author—Michael Cox—has gone on to work for the ABC in the area of church planting. And the other author—Joe Ratliff—has continued to increase in visibility as senior pastor of one of the SBC's largest congregations. We are in good positions to understand what many denominations are doing in the way of starting churches. Since the original publication of this book, we have both seen ecumenical endeavors and experiences increase, and so we believe the need for this book is greater than ever.

The publication of the first edition also permitted the authors to lecture and lead workshops in a variety of non-Baptist settings that affirmed the need for this revision and for doing it with a greater sense of inclusion, beyond the Baptist community. This does not decrease the strong Baptist influence, but it does broaden the authors' perspectives and affirm their conclusions.

The Odds against a Successful Journey

The same conviction drives us on our journey today as that drove us when we were preparing the first edition of this book. Our journey, simply put, is to start churches in predominantly black communities.

The journey sounds simple, but consider the odds.

First, such a journey puts us at odds with our Protestant history. Protestants have long upheld the belief that blacks had souls and were capable of being saved—if "they" stayed comfortably and innocuously in "their" churches. Is this the same belief that today is launching an aggressive campaign to start churches in black communities?

Second, such a journey puts us at odds with the reigning culture. Although blacks and whites are at least theoretically treated as equals, a quiet racism threatens to rock us into complacency. Consider the facts: African American men outnumber white men in our prisons. A significantly smaller percentage of black young people graduate from college as compared to white young people. And a significantly higher percentage of black families live in poverty as compared to white families. We could make still more such comparisons.

Racial equality seems to be the exception rather than the norm. Is this culture ready for any denomination to enter predominantly black communities to start churches?

Third, such a journey puts us at odds with popular theology. Despite all of our protests to the contrary, popular theology does not practically embrace the heterogeneous-unit principle (the idea that a local church body can flourish while representing a variety of ethnicities and other kinds of diversity). Eleven o'clock on Sunday morning is still the most segregated hour during the week.

Keep in mind that we are proposing starting churches in predominantly black communities, not starting black churches. There is a difference, however subtle it may appear.

Is our theology open enough to sometimes forgo what has defensively been called "human nature" to follow God's nature?

Fourth, such a journey puts us at odds with contemporary political maneuverings. As blacks, who have long been politically downtrodden, become a national force to be reckoned with, the call for "common ground" becomes a cheer for one-race tickets. If you vote for someone from your own ethnic background, you are promised that you will be the beneficiary. Such jockeying for political power and position contradicts religious leaders' vocal commitment to justice. Is the political establishment far enough removed from our religious world that the two shall never meet? Or does there need to be more acting and less talking from both the religious and the political worlds about "liberty and justice for all"?

Fifth, such a journey puts us at odds with calculations of economic feasibility. In today's world the bottom line is what counts. With accountant-type accuracy, we calculate the relative success or failure of any venture, even church starting. To start churches in black communities means that some will never be successful by contemporary standards. Some of these churches must be started in ghettoes or in housing projects. These churches may never be self-supporting; they may never be large. Are we ready to put away the tally sheets and announce, "Whatever the cost, we are willing"?

Sixth, such a journey puts us at odds with socially acceptable behavior. Many see predominantly white denominations as holding out the carrots of financial and resource assistance to struggling black churches. Traditional black churches have been accused of not having the resources to do what must be done to reach America's black population for Christ. Are traditional white denominations and traditional black denominations willing to quit bickering and make it socially acceptable for blacks and whites to work together to reach the unreached, whatever their race? (This does not even speak to the presence of people representing other ethnicities, such as Hispanics and Asians. When you factor them in, it makes working together even more complex.)

Yes, the odds seem to be against us. But with the conviction that what we are doing is inspired by God, the odds are surmountable.

THE PURPOSE OF THIS BOOK

That's what this book is about—overcoming the odds.

The ABC has a national goal of starting 1,010 new churches of all kinds by the year 2010. (It does not, however, have a strategy for reaching or starting a specific number of black churches.) Since becoming the director of new church planting in the ABC's National Ministries division, Michael Cox has helped develop each of the thirty-four ABC regions in promoting grassroots strategies that project new starts and target unreached people groups. The regions are beginning to act on these strategies, and this action will become the basis for the national ABC activity in church planting.

The history in the ABC has not been strong in developing intentional grassroots strategies for new church planting.

However, if the denomination is to be successful in the planting of 1,010 new churches by 2010, such strategies are essential. National organizations have the role of casting the vision, facilitating strategy development, and discovering and developing resources. They cannot, however, plant a church from the national headquarters, because, in the long run, the pursuit of the church-starting vision is best done as close to the new church as possible.

This book answers the "Why?" and the "How?" of reaching an often misunderstood, seemingly impossible, and unpopular goal. *The purpose of this book is to present a theology and strategy for church planting and growth in the black community.*

Notice the little article "a" in that purpose statement. This book purports nothing more and nothing less than to present *a* theology and strategy. It would be folly to attempt to try to present *the* theology and strategy.

As the authors of this book, we have strong convictions about our theology and strategy of church planting. But we recognize that situations, and thus strategies, vary and that people's perceptions of theology mature and evolve. Much of the theology and strategy presented here unapologetically come as a direct result of the church experiences of the authors and of our having grown up in the Southern Baptist Convention. Over time, our experiences have changed our outlook.

Accept this book in its purest intentions—as a theology and strategy.

REASONS FOR THIS BOOK

Why do we need a theology and strategy for church planting and growth in the black community? Several reasons are evident. We're going to look at three: the lack of intentionality in church starting in black areas, the high percentage of unchurched African Americans, and the scarcity of resources on this topic. We could state other reasons for articulating a strategy and theology for church planting and growth in the black community. However, for the purpose of this book, the three selected reasons seem to be the most overarching and pertinent.

The Lack of Intentionality in Church Starting

In the past, church starting in black communities lacked intentionality. Churches seemed to appear, and sometimes disappear, overnight. There is a plausible explanation for why church planting and growth in black communities have so long been on the back burner of the national denominations.

Historically, for black people, the church was all in all. The black church helped to define and defend black culture. The black church provided a sense of equality and dignity to those who were downtrodden in everyday living. Perhaps the most important gift that the historical black church offered its constituents was a theology of hope not only for the hereafter but also for day-to-day living.

Because of the centrality of the church in black people's lives, its existence and propagation were natural. There was no question that, in one form or another, the church would be where the people were. The church just happened. Church planting was informal and sometimes spontaneous. If a new church was needed, it was started. Churches were begun and grown with as little interference from whites as possible.

But through the years, the role of the church in the black community has changed. No longer is it all in all. While the black church still offers a theology of hope, blacks have other arenas in which to work for justice, to build families, to be entertained, to learn. Thus the church is not as much a natural outgrowth of people's lives as it was in the past. The church doesn't just happen anymore; it must be made to happen. To meet today's challenges and needs for churches in black communities, we must deliberately and prayerfully seek locations, invest resources, and persevere until a congregation is begun.

The Number of Unchurched Blacks

The second reason why a theology and strategy for church planting and growth in black communities are desperately needed is related to the first reason. A large number of blacks are what researchers label as "unchurched."

In March 1988 the Gallup organization conducted a national religious survey of the adult population in America. According to this study, 40 percent of all blacks in

America are unchurched. Ten years later, in 1998, the Gallup poll indicated that one in three African Americans are considered unchurched. In this more recent survey, the definition of "unchurched" encompassed "those who are not members of a church, or who have not attended services in the previous six months other than for special religious holidays, weddings, funerals, or the like."[2] (The 1988 poll included church members who had not attended church in the past six months. This accounts for the difference between the 40 percent in 1988 and the 32 percent in 1998.) It must be noted that the percentage of unchurched blacks did not differ significantly from the percentages of unchurched whites and Hispanics.

In 1999 a survey by George Barna reported that only 49 percent of African Americans attend church on any given Sunday, and 21 percent of African Americans consider themselves to be unchurched (a term that was not defined in the survey).[3] The statistic concerning church attendance is useful and informative for the purpose of new church planting. It, in combination with the 2000 census data that estimates the total population of blacks in America at well over 34 million, indicates that there is plenty of work yet to be done in the African American community.[4]

Interestingly, 86 percent of all surveyed blacks indicated that religion was at least "fairly important" to them. This includes 69 percent of the unchurched blacks. In response to a question directed specifically to the unchurched who at one time had been more active in church than they were presently, 73 percent of blacks indicated a possibility that they would become "fairly active members of a church or synagogue." These statistics seem to imply that something may be missing from existing black churches. It also seems to indicate that a high number of unchurched blacks would be good prospects for church membership.

The next question becomes "Why are the unchurched unchurched?" Reasons are many and varied. However, one fairly reliable indicator has to do with attitude toward organized religion. Here the differences among respondents in different racial groups are more pronounced. Fifty-one percent of blacks, as compared to 40 percent of both whites and Hispanics, were concerned about what they consider to be the churches' insufficient concern with social justice issues. Further, 70 percent of blacks agreed that "one church is as good as another," as compared to 60 percent of Hispanics and 54 percent of whites. While attitude toward organized religion is not the only indicator for why people do not attend, it is a fairly accurate barometer of where people are at.

Since the first edition of this book, the members of Generation X have thrown some new factors into the mix. This generation seems to have a unique take on church and spirituality. Historically, in the black community we assumed that everyone either went to church or had some church experience. The black church was the center of the community. Although the church is still central in the community, the number of people dependent on the church has decreased. Fewer members of this Gen X group seek solutions from the church. They consider themselves spiritual but don't consider the church as the primary option for their spiritual journey.

The Lack of Resources on the Topic

A third reason why there is a desperate need for a theology and strategy for church planting and growth in the black community is because of a conspicuous lack of written resources on the topic. A bibliography of resources related to religion in black America is included at the end of this book. These resources are commendable and insightful. However, even a cursory scan of these resources indicates a dearth of information on church planting and growth in the black community.

The lack of such resources is certainly not an oversight. It is a testimony to the place to which church planting and growth have been relegated in the black community. Church planting and growth in the black community have not been high priorities; now, they must become so.

THE TARGET AUDIENCE OF THIS BOOK

The target audience of this book is you. Whether you are a black or white pastor of a Southern Baptist, American Baptist, or National Baptist church, a leader in your denominational convention, a seminary student or professor, a minister or leader in another evangelical denomination, or a layperson, this book is for you.

The targeting of this book has intentionally been kept as wide and as open as possible. The reason for that is simple: church planting and growth in black communities do not belong to any one group. Enough lost people live in these communities for everyone to be concerned. It would be arrogant for any group to pretend that they "owned" or had exclusive rights to evangelize those lost people based upon the color of their skin. We must all be concerned and active in reaching into these black communities and sharing Christ with the residents.

Because the audience is so broad, few generalizations can be made. However, the authors have made at least one assumption about the book's readers. That is, if you are reading this book, you are at least nominally interested in church planting in black communities. That interest may be influenced by any number of factors, such as seeking credit in a class or just plain being curious. But whatever the influence, the interest is there. The authors hope to take that interest and add to it some information that can help it grow.

THE CONTENTS OF THIS BOOK

Because this book presents an overall theology and strategy for church planting in the black community, it is organized topically, not chronologically or sequentially as in a how-to book. In selecting and discussing topics the authors have tried to consider and answer in advance various questions that people interested in starting and growing churches in black communities might ask.

Chapter two examines nine church starts in which the authors were directly involved. What lessons do these church starts offer to a congregation willing to start a new church? What lessons do they offer to members of a new church wanting to become better established?

Chapter three speaks to the matter of taking your interest or vision for church planting in the black community and translating it into action. Why would anyone want to start churches in black communities? How can one determine if there is really a need for a new church in a particular community? How can various people, such as a potential sponsoring pastor, a local community leader, a church planter, or church members, be inspired to buy in to the vision and need for a new church?

Chapter four presents an understanding of the role of the sponsoring church. What types of churches would make appropriate sponsors for churches in black communities? Where can these church sponsors be found? How is the relationship between the sponsoring church and new church developed? What responsibilities does the church sponsor have to accept? When does the relationship between the church sponsor and new church end?

Chapter five presents an understanding of the church planter. What motivates a church planter? What keeps a church planter on the job when he or she must often face a low church budget, a low salary, low attendance, and low visibility? What role does the church planter fulfill in the new congregation? What kind of commitment must she or he make to the new congregation?

Chapter six identifies several common pitfalls to avoid in starting churches in black communities. Is the new congregation playing the numbers game? Is the new congregation looking out for number one? How does the new congregation make decisions? Where does the new congregation fit into the big picture? Is the new congregation "rehearsing" or "reversing" when it comes to social ills? Is the new congregation standing its ground? Is the new congregation thinking about tomorrow? Is the new congregation trying to go it alone?

HOW TO USE THIS BOOK

The information in this book will help the person truly interested in starting and growing churches in black communities. However, there is something that is significantly more important than any information presented here. That is how the reader uses the information.

Obviously, this is not a coffee-table book, intended to look inviting and be entertaining. This is a book intended to spur its readers on to action. Consider the following ideas for making the most of your reading experience.

Read the book thoughtfully. If you're going to spend time reading this book, then spend it wisely. Try to keep distractions to a minimum while you read. Hold a pen in your hand as you're reading. Underline anything that makes you think, that makes you nod your head in agreement, or that makes you angry. Jot down notes and questions in the margins.

Read the footnotes. Some quotes or thoughts borrowed from others here will intrigue you. Find the sources. Read the quotes or thoughts in context.

Read the bibliography. It was not put in the book just to fill blank pages. The listed books come from a variety of authors and publishers and speak to a variety of topics. They represent the best in the field. Select a few to read and add to your library.

Talk to others. After you've read the book, or even as you are reading, talk to others about the ideas you've encountered. Flip back through the book, noticing what you underlined or questions you jotted down. Share your insights or questions with those whom you respect. Ask their opinions and insights.

Do something. After reading the book, make an intentional decision to do something about what you've read. Don't put the book aside and forget about it; act on it. Your act might be as simple as giving the book to somebody else to read or as monumental as leading your congregation to sponsor a church in a black community. It doesn't matter so much what the act is, as long as you take some kind of positive steps.

CONCLUSION

We are preparing for our journey in church planting in black communities. We are packing our bags and buckling our seat belts. The journey will not end with the last page of this book. In fact, that is when the journey truly begins. Where will *your* journey take *you*?

Notes
1. *The basic outline describing Jesus' journey through Samaria comes from an address given by Otis Moss Jr. at Emory University, Atlanta, Georgia, on September 18, 1990.*
2. *Gallup Organization website: www.gallup.com.*
3. *Barna Research website: www.barna.org.*
4. *U.S. Census Bureau, Census 2000 (Public Law 94-171), summary file, tables PL1, PL2.*

CHAPTER 2

Learning from Those Who Have Gone Before

THE JOURNEY CONTINUES. ALONG THE WAY WE WILL experience indescribable joys and heartaches. We will have Sundays that we wish could go on forever and Sundays that we would just as soon forget.

Such are the ups and downs, twists and turns of our journey toward planting churches in black communities. As we journey through each of these experiences, we are reminded that many have gone before us, allowing their faith to take them to worlds unknown. Their faith has taken them to black communities where others have not dared to go. Their faith has led them to start churches when the odds were against them.

These predecessors become our teachers. They serve as our inspiration. They cheer us on. They help to light our way at its darkest moments. And when the light reappears, they are there with us, uttering a prayer of thanksgiving.

At times they shout at us; at times they whisper. Yet the message is the same: "It can be done!"

NINE CASE STUDIES IN CHURCH PLANTING

This chapter will examine church starts in black communities in which the two authors were directly related.

Eight of the church starts are located in the Houston, Texas. Each of these churches was sponsored, at least in part, by Brentwood Baptist Church. Brentwood—the largest black church in the Southern Baptist Convention—welcomes approximately five thousand upper-middle-class people to its worship services each Sunday morning. Joe Ratliff has served as pastor of Brentwood since 1980.

The other church start, in Euclid, Ohio, was led by Michael Cox. Michael served as the first black church planter apprentice of the Home Mission Board, Southern Baptist Convention, from 1984 to 1988.

Case Study I:
First Baptist Greens Bayou, Houston, Texas

People grieving over their neighbors who had left the neighborhood, daring to hold worship services when the pews and parking lot were close to empty, resorting to using day-care receipts to pay their beloved pastor. Such was the situation of First Baptist Greens Bayou in 1984. "White flight" had forced a significant transition in the traditionally white middle-class community in north Houston. Frightened church members and their resources left their neighborhoods and their church in droves.

Ten to twelve stalwart members and the pastor stayed. Some members even commuted to their church from other neighborhoods. They were determined. They didn't want to lose their Southern Baptist witness in the community that had been their home for so many years.

Yet the church was reeling from the blows. The only thing that seemed to be working for the church was its day-care center. While the adults were nervous about the church's future, you could still see children jumping rope with a carefree abandon, daring each other to go down the slide headfirst, and scurrying into a not-so-straight line when the familiar whistle sounded. The day-care center still attracted neighborhood residents, while the church apparently could not.

Brentwood heard of First Baptist Greens Bayou's plight. Sometime earlier Brentwood had entered an agreement with Union Baptist Association that the association would inform Brentwood of any church in significant transition and in danger of closing its doors. Brentwood's intent was pure—to ensure that a Southern Baptist witness would remain in the community and that the church facility would not be sold to the highest bidder.

Acting as much as a consultant as a sponsoring church, Brentwood assisted First Baptist Greens Bayou in assessing its situation and making the transition from being a church in a predominantly white community to one in a predominantly black community. The white pastor knew what was happening to his community and, when the time came, he was willing to step aside and allow others to continue to build upon the Christian witness he had begun. For three months, two pastors served the church—one, the original white pastor; the other, a newly recruited black pastor.

In a history-making event a constitution service was held, commemorating the church's change of leadership and constituency. The church kept its name and its affiliation with the Southern Baptist Convention. The white pastor moved on to another pastorate; the black pastor took over leadership of the church.

With his personality, people skills, and organizational ability, the new pastor, Rev. M. E. Williams, canvassed his neighborhood, where most of the people were new residents without a church home, and told them about First Baptist Greens Bayou. Under its new black leadership, the church grew from an initial nine members to almost two hundred in its first year and more than a thousand in its fourth year.

Rev. Williams retired in 1988, and Rev. Robert Dixson was called as pastor. The young congregation lost members during the initial pastoral transition, but today the congregation is strong and growing, with membership numbers exceeding fifteen hundred.

Case Study 2:
End Time Baptist Church, Houston, Texas

It is Sunday morning. People are streaming from every direction; they are heading in the same direction—toward Brentwood Baptist Church's massive domed sanctuary. A few, however, are not going into the dome. Instead they are entering Brentwood's smaller chapel. Once inside, they smile at one another. They embrace. They have found a home, their home—End Time Baptist Church, a Brentwood mission.

Begun originally as a Bible study, End Time had a specific target group—blacks with Caribbean ancestry. The small group began meeting with Brentwood for Sunday morning worship services but soon felt a desire to have a church of their own, in which they could enjoy the Caribbean worship style. Although the people starting End Time were black, they had a different cultural identification than Brentwood's members. Thus the need for a separate church.

Rather than feeling threatened, Brentwood affirmed End Time's need to have an identity of its own. Brentwood offered the use of its chapel, free of charge, for two years. During that time (1984 to 1986), the group went from about twenty to about seventy-five people. Brentwood then assisted the congregation in locating and renting a day-care center for its worship services. After using the day-care facility through 1989, the church moved to the pastor's home for one year. Ultimately, the church purchased a three-room house and converted it into a church building. With a membership today of approximately four hundred, the church continues to grow and has matured under the leadership of three pastors. The current pastor, Rev. Melvin Wells, has served since 1998.

Case Study 3:
St. Paul Baptist Church, Houston, Texas

Fried chicken, ham, baked beans, potato salad, congealed salad, chocolate cake. Sounds like a family reunion or the ever-popular dinner on the grounds. In this case, however, it is a kickoff event for a new church, St. Paul Baptist Church.

Begun in 1986 under the joint sponsorship of Brentwood and an Anglo church in north Houston, St. Paul reaches upper-middle-class blacks. Many erroneously assume that a black community necessarily is a low-income area. St. Paul puts that assumption to rest. St. Paul is located in The Woodlands, a planned community of homes starting at around $200,000, just north of Houston.

Reaching upper-income people, whether black or white, means using different methods than those used in reaching lower-income people. An example is St. Paul's kickoff picnic. In The Woodlands most of the residents commute daily the approximately thirty miles to Houston to work. Once they are home in the evening, they rarely venture out to socialize or meet neighbors. The picnic offered community residents an opportunity not only to learn about the new church but also to become acquainted with their neighbors.

Advertised through telephone calls, through professionally printed flyers and letters, and by word of mouth, the picnic attracted a good group. As a result of the picnic, twelve people began meeting for Bible study at the home of Jimmy Dotson, Houston's deputy chief of police. The congregation soon moved to the community's interfaith center for its "Baptist hour." (Other denominations worshiped in that same facility at different hours.) In its first year St. Paul grew to fifty-six people, and today, in its seventh year, it attracts approximately 350 people to its worship services.

The church has a good economic base because its members' incomes are high and because the congregation saved money while worshiping in the interfaith center. Thus the congregation was able to purchase six acres of land on which to build its own facility. The finished building seats more than two hundred worshipers. Michael Cox served this congregation as interim pastor in 1998 and 1999, and the current pastor is Rev. Frank McGee Jr.

Case Study 4:
Greenspoint Baptist Church, Houston, Texas

Take a husband-and-wife team, both of them trained at seminary, along with ten or so couples from Brentwood.

Provide generous start-up funds. Wait a short while. The result? Greenspoint Baptist Church, begun in 1986, founded by Rev. Jimmy and Denise Wilson. In five years, this new church had reached a membership of approximately twelve hundred. In 1991, the Wilson's pastorate was followed by a vacant pulpit for nearly eighteen months, at which point the Rev. Robert Menefee assumed the helm. Struggling through the usual challenges of following a successful, founding pastorate, the church's growth plateaued and declined. Under the current pastor, Rev. Victor Williams, the congregation has rebounded, built a facility that seats more than one thousand, and numbers a thriving membership of more than two thousand.

In north Houston another community was in racial transition. Like the Greens Bayou neighborhood, this community was moving from being predominantly white to being predominantly black. Losing its white constituency, the community maintained its economic stability with the newly arriving blacks.

Union Baptist Association viewed this changing community as an opportunity rather than as a problem. When Brentwood was approached with the possibility of starting a church in this newly emerging black community, it responded not just with dollars but also with people. In investing approximately twenty-five of its members to start Greenspoint, Brentwood has reached more than a thousand people who otherwise might not have been reached.

Case Study 5:
Faith Baptist Church, Houston, Texas

Too often, a church split means only pain and misunderstanding. Yet Faith Baptist Church, which began as a split from another church, moved beyond its pain and misunderstanding. It now is a positive and growing influence for Christ in its community.

Faith began with a handful of members meeting in a hotel for several months. With an emphasis on lifestyle evangelism, community ministry, and visitation and canvassing, the church soon became too large for its hotel home.

Faith's pastor, Rev. Alvin Molten, was an aggressive, self-made man, and he knew a facility had to be found. With no Southern Baptist background, Molten still knew of Brentwood's church-starting reputation. Molten approached Brentwood with a plea for assistance. Brentwood leaders had never heard of the young church planter or of Faith Church until Molten called to set up an appointment. Molten's people skills and obvious dream won him a hearing. Brentwood heard his presentation, did the necessary research to ascertain the validity of his claims, and agreed to the sponsorship.

One of Brentwood's first tasks as a new sponsor was to help Faith find a suitable location for its growing congregation. An Anglo congregation was vacating its facility in the suburbs, and this soon became the home for Faith.

Another significant task for Brentwood has been educating Molten in what it means to be Southern Baptist. Since his first contact with Brentwood, the church planter has become an active contributor to the Baptist association.

Begun in 1987 with thirty-seven people, in 2001, Faith boasts eleven hundred members and is still thriving under the continuing leadership of Rev. Molten. In fact, the congregation has relocated to a suburban facility to accommodate their growth.

Case Study 6:
Bissonnet Baptist Church, Houston, Texas

A few miles west of Houston's inner city, a stark warehouse provides a meeting place for Bissonnet Baptist Church, another mission of Brentwood Baptist Church.[1] Begun in November 1989 as a home Bible study with only thirteen members, in 2001 the mission now includes more than six hundred members.

Pastor Steve Crampton, who won the Home Mission Board's church planter of the year award in 1991, says his "spiritual intuition" led him to consider starting a church in this community, a racially transitional neighborhood with no black church. Initial discussions with Union Baptist Association directed the young church planter to Brentwood Baptist, which assisted him in conducting a feasibility study of the area.

Most of the members are African Americans in their mid to late thirties. Most seem to be fairly comfortable financially. Others are not. The mission has earmarked 10 percent of each Sunday's offering to help those in need.

Transforming the warehouse into a church has put the congregation's carpentry skills to the test. One deacon has led work crews to install bathrooms, pews, and seats and to repair and paint the concrete floor.

Originally Crampton wanted to purchase the entire warehouse and renovate it into a school, using adjacent property to build the church facility. And he wanted to buy nearby apartments to offer low-income housing to neighborhood residents. However, Crampton and the church seized another opportunity recently and purchased an existing church facility that seats eight hundred. Through many struggles, this congregation today averages four hundred in worship, and Pastor Crampton is still a visionary.

He shares his plans at every opportunity, even in sermons. "When you realize your reward, you don't have any small plans anymore," he says. Spontaneous clapping emerges from the congregation. They are with him, big plans and all.

Case Study 7:
Heart of Houston Church, Houston, Texas

On the outskirts of what is known as the fourth ward, one of Houston's most impoverished, crime-ridden areas, shiny late-model cars turned into the parking lot of Grace Theater, headquarters for a Christian troupe, The A.D. Players.

The one hundred or so people who emerged from the cars and made their way toward the theater were casually attired, mostly young, and mostly white. Inside they greeted one another warmly, sang Christian choruses accompanied by a guitar, and listened intently as Pastor Doug Tipps spoke into a standing microphone.

The theater housed Heart of Houston Church, a new church plant that eventually failed. Although the atmosphere was casual, the worship service moved like clockwork. It had to. The mission rented the theater by the hour.

Begun earlier as a home Bible study, this mission was the product of a dream. For ten years, Tipps served as pastor of Houston's River Oaks Baptist Church, a large, wealthy Anglo church. He and his family lived two blocks from a country club and for a while were neighbors of former Texas governor John Connally.

But Tipps became convinced that Southern Baptists were "running from the inner city," leaving entire downtown areas "leavenless." Tipps' dream began to take shape. He wanted to start a church that would reach people of all races and economic backgrounds, a church that would "address the problems only churches can address." He wanted to start a church that would "recontextualize the gospel," speaking when and where it wasn't expected.

And he didn't want to start a church sponsored by a white, racially homogeneous church. "We would never be able to overcome our parentage," he explained.

Tipps found a sponsor in Brentwood Church. For Brentwood, sponsorship of Heart of Houston meant including the pastor and his family on its group insurance plan; helping the church find a suitable location; and offering support, challenge, and encouragement as needed. After finding the necessary sponsorship, Tipps sold his home in the affluent neighborhood, purchased a more modest home, and began the new church.

In addition to intentionally finding a black sponsoring church, Heart of Houston was also intentional in ensuring that church leadership was balanced racially and economically. The church aimed to develop a core group of middle- and upper-middle-class people "looking for significance." Many of the early members had not attended church in years. They began to take hold of Tipps' dream, entering inner-city neighborhoods to hold prayer meetings in the streets, adopting schools, and helping to rebuild families.

Tipps knew building his dream church wouldn't be easy. But he was determined to foster in Heart of Houston a church that would be "deeply in love with the city."

In time, what Tipps, Brentwood, and others realized was that this kind of church planting requires more than idealized notions. Within two years of attempting this multicultural church plant, Tipps closed the doors. The endeavor had failed.

The failure was attributable to several dynamics. First, the vision, though admirable, included too broad a target audience. This made it difficult to put together a focused vision path leading to success. Second, having a multicultural leadership team is just not enough to bring about success in this kind of plant. Outside of California, there were few known multicultural church plants from which to gain substantial, experiential information about what should, could, shouldn't, and couldn't be done. Spanning the racial divide between African Americans and white Americans takes more than an abstract vision. Add to this dynamic the complexity of the economic divisions Tipps wanted to cross, and it meant the strategy deployed in this plant had little chance at success.

And in the final analysis, Tipps could not cross the divide on a personal level. As an individual, he just couldn't sell this vision to enough poor whites and blacks he earnestly wanted to reach. A critical mass from this significant portion of the target audience was not convinced that this church was an option for them.

Case Study 8:
Southwest Community Baptist Church, Houston, Texas

In a western suburb of Houston, bivocational pastor Gregg Patrick is putting his real estate skills to work in his church. Patrick negotiated the purchase of an entire shopping center for Southwest Community Baptist Church to use as its home.

Southwest Community Baptist Church began in 1991 with a nucleus of nineteen people in a home Bible study led by Patrick. Within a year, the church averaged one hundred people in its worship service. Many of the additions have come through the pastor's door-to-door witnessing.

Today, the church has built a center for worship services

that seats fifteen hundred; membership exceeds four thousand. Plans include using the 27,900-square-foot complex to house a community center with a Christian academy and day care, cultural arts gallery, Christian bookstore, musical arts school and gospel music center, and soul food restaurant.

Rev. Patrick sees the community center as just one way to reach the people.

Many did not understand the need for a new black Southern Baptist church in this quickly developing community, which is only 17 percent black. But Patrick did. To him that 17 percent represents about fifty thousand people, most of whom are in two-career, white-collar families bringing home upper-middle-class salaries. Most, according to Patrick, are "unchurched believers." If he has his way, they won't be unchurched for long.

Brentwood's sponsorship of Southwest Community involves little financial support. Primarily the sponsorship involves a sharing of lay leadership as needed. For example, the Brentwood Women's Missionary Union director offered assistance in starting a Women's Missionary Union.

Case Study 9:
Faith Community Baptist Church, Euclid, Ohio

The community of Euclid, Ohio, just northeast of Cleveland, boasts a population of seventy-two thousand, including five thousand blacks.[2] Two Southern Baptist churches, Willoughby and Mount Calvary (now First Baptist South Euclid) decided their community needed more than one predominantly black church.

To speak to that need, Willoughby members started a bus ministry. But soon they discovered that they were reaching children instead of entire families. "We were trying to find a way to reach black adults because we were only reaching children," says former Willoughby pastor Lynton Younger. So the church began a home Bible study and eventually called Michael Cox, a then-recent graduate of Southwestern Baptist Theological Seminary, as church starter.

Cox's first order of business was to determine why two well-intentioned white churches faced such difficulty in starting a predominantly black church. The answer—pragmatically understandable but theologically questionable—was simple: people go to church where they feel comfortable, where there are people like them.

When Cox took over the reins of the home Bible study, it had seven members, of whom four were white. Within two months, the group had increased to twenty members.

Thus began Faith's struggle to find a suitable location. During its first six months, Faith was forced to relocate three times. The first meeting place beyond the home was an American Baptist church, but the rental agreement lasted only four weeks. While in its American Baptist home, Faith planned a special worship event with a well-known, national figure—Martin Luther King III. Advertised in newspapers and on the radio, that event attracted 120 people but cost Faith its home.

Faith's next location option was Mount Calvary, one of its sponsoring churches. Mount Calvary planned to sell its facilities and merge with another Baptist church. Faith was not interested in buying the building but offered to rent it. Instead, Mount Calvary sold its facilities to the nearby black Evangelical Christian Church. So Faith relocated to a local elementary school.

By its first anniversary, Faith could afford to buy or build but could not find a suitable building or land. The church found a vacant lot in the heart of Euclid, but the acreage was zoned for apartments or single-family use. Petitioning the city council to rezone the land for church use, Faith was turned down. The land was sold to a used-car dealership that went bankrupt.

Despite its many setbacks related to finding a suitable location, Faith survived and grew. The first year for Faith was one of survival, including a period of spiritual and numerical depression. The second year was marked by spiritual growth—an unplanned, unscheduled revival. Concentrating less on numerical growth and more on leadership and Sunday school, Cox freed the church to begin expecting great things of itself. Faith Community Baptist Church started with faith, survived with faith, and has continued to grow with faith.

Faith Community has thrived even more under the pastorate of Rev. Michael Perryman. It now has a worship facility that seats more than four hundred.

TEN LESSONS FROM THE CASE STUDIES

A cursory examination of the nine church starts presented in this chapter confirms much of what will be extensively discussed in the following chapters of this book. But for now, consider the following major points:

1. The right church starter is a key to the success of a new church. While the church starter has to have vision, drive, and commitment for the new church, he or she doesn't necessarily have to meet external qualifications, such as a certain level of education, ordination, or the desire to be a full-time minister. Too often, insisting that a church planter have certain external qualifications actually impedes the church-starting venture by disqualifying individuals who would be excellent church starters. Many of the church starters in the new churches featured in this chapter were not Southern Baptist or seminary-trained before starting a Southern Baptist church. They did not meet "textbook requirements." But often these were the best church starters for the situation because they had a heart for the task. They learned and fulfilled the external qualifications as they fulfilled their vision of building a church.

2. The new church must be creative and flexible when it comes to facilities. Too often new church planters believe that just getting a building will solve the problem of how to reach people. It will not. If a church planter does not have an emphasis on reaching people and a quality ministry focus, a building will mean little if anything. With the nine churches of the case studies, facilities included a warehouse, a hotel, a day-care center, a sponsoring church's chapel, a school, a shopping center, and an interfaith center. Church starters or sponsors who force a church into a debt-ridden building program too soon may pay the price for years to come. Innovative use of existing buildings generally serves the community as well as the kingdom of God.

3. Different methods reach different people. The picnic that St. Paul Baptist Church used to introduce its church was target-group specific. So were the kickoff events of other churches in the case studies, though those events were quite different. Church starters must know the communities in which they want to build churches. They must know the people and their needs. Without such crucial knowledge, church starters would be ill equipped to use the appropriate outreach methods for their communities.

4. The necessary resources include more than money. While they think most often in terms of money, sponsoring churches have many other resources to offer the new church. Some of the resources that Brentwood offered new churches in the case studies included counsel, lay leadership, ministerial leadership, education, facilities, and so forth. Each one was crucial.

5. The sponsoring church must take a businesslike approach. Because Brentwood Baptist Church did not know Alvin Molten or his church, it approached his request for assistance pragmatically and carefully. A church that actively sponsors one or more new churches will gain a reputation. It will be approached frequently with requests for assistance and sponsorship. It is appropriate to hear each request but not to respond positively to each. Many kind and generous sponsoring churches have felt the pain of betrayal or the drain of emotional and financial resources. Sponsoring churches, while open to the Holy Spirit's leadership, must do their homework before agreeing to sponsor a new church.

6. The sponsoring church must have a vision for the kingdom of God. A sponsoring church that is busy guarding its own turf has little to offer a new church. Established and new churches both must have an attitude that says, "We're in this together." When Brentwood Baptist Church "gave" twenty-five of its members to Greenspoint, the kingdom of God gained nearly a thousand citizens in return.

7. The sponsoring church can sponsor more than one church at a time. Although Brentwood did not sponsor all eight churches in the case studies simultaneously, it did sponsor several churches at one time. Sponsorship of several churches concurrently is possible because sponsorship should mean something different in each situation. Sponsorship often, but not always, means financial commitment. Where sponsorship does not involve large financial commitments, such as in Brentwood Baptist Church's sponsorship of Southwestern Community Baptist Church, the sponsoring church is able to sponsor more than one church simultaneously.

Ten Lessons from the Case Studies

8. A new church must be accountable to its sponsoring church and vice versa. Accountability should be built into the covenant between the new church and the sponsoring church. The new church and sponsoring church are in a partnership to reach people for Christ. Brentwood Baptist Church was holding Heart of Houston Baptist Church pastor Doug Tipps accountable to his dream of a racially and economically balanced team of church leaders. Brentwood was also doing its part to help make that dream a reality, even until its eventual closing.

9. The development of lay leadership should be a top priority for any new church. As churches grow, the pastors quickly learn that they cannot do everything. Pastors must believe in word and deed that each layperson is a minister. A church limits itself if it does not equip its laypeople. Faith Baptist Church members enter their community to witness and minister. Much of what the members do could not be accomplished by the pastor. They reach out to their neighbors and friends, and the church grows.

10. The longer the tenure of the pastor, the greater the likelihood of success for the church. In each of the case-study churches, when a pastor left, numbers dwindled, at least temporarily. Although many of the churches ultimately regained the numbers lost, some of the individuals following the pastor were never regained. Pastors should be encouraged to stick with it, to live out their commitment. Sponsoring churches can point new church pastors to the broader vision of the kingdom of God when circumstances seem insurmountable. Regular dialogue between the sponsoring church and the church planter is essential in retention. Setting goals that are realistic and achievable while seeking input to solutions from the sponsoring church and mentors will aid the planter in staying the course. Few if any planters plant with no challenges at hand.

CONCLUSION

The churches presented in this chapter have gone before us. They have demonstrated that, despite whatever obstacles may present themselves in the course of planting a church in a black community, it can be done!

Notes

1. *Case studies six, seven, and eight are based upon Margaret Dempsey, "Brentwood: Building Churches from Dreams," Mis-*sionsUSA *(Atlanta: Home Mission Board, September–October 1991), 36–40.*
2. *Case study nine is based upon Leisa A. Hammett, "Turn Me Loose, Let Me Go,"* MissionsUSA, *57, no. 5 (September–October 1986):5–13.*

CHAPTER 3

Sharpening a Vision for Church Planting

IN THE LAST CHAPTER WE SAW EXAMPLES OF HOW OTHERS have journeyed down the road toward starting churches in black communities. But our journey must also begin with a vision of what could be but does not yet exist. This vision must be God-given, and it must reign supreme. Even when everything surrounding the vision—such as budget, facilities, and resources—seems to be working against it, the vision can continue to inspire and drive us in planting a church.

One critical mistake many church planters make is to sacrifice their vision for the sake of a model. We are "model hungry." Numerous model conferences are planned annually. Would-be church planters flock to these conferences, diligently taking notes and making a to-do list in their heads of how to go home and replicate that model in their communities.

Yet such a strategy doesn't work over the long haul. Models are important; they are created and designed to bring a vision to reality. Yet models are not supreme. The vision is supreme.

Many a church planter has given up in despair when the chosen model ceases to work, when it ceases to reach people. Yet if a vision were foundational for the church planter, that individual would realize that a model can change. In spite of the model change, the vision can remain constant.

An example of vision driving a new church start was Heart of Houston Baptist Church, a failed mission of Brentwood Baptist Church. Mission pastor Doug Tipps's vision was to start an inner-city church for people of all races and economic backgrounds—one that would proclaim the gospel when and where it was not expected. His model for fulfilling his vision included renting a neutral location accessible to the people he wanted to reach, developing a racially balanced church staff, and performing ministry in the inner city. Yet such models are expendable. When one proves fruitless, it can be replaced by a more appropriate model. For example, if Tipps had discovered that the location used for the church was attracting only one segment of the audience he had hoped to attract, he could have systematically discovered why that particular location was not working and found a more suitable location.

One actual trouble faced by this church was that, at first, the vision was not supported by a realistic understanding of how difficult accomplishing the vision would be. It is important to balance what we believe our God-given vision is with a realistic understanding of the facts that will impact our success.

The vision becomes the driving force behind decision making about which models are to be tried and used, which are to never be tried, and which are to be tried and discarded.

This chapter addresses how to develop and sharpen such a vision so that it is what moves and motivates us in our church-planting task. Several key elements contribute to the overall vision of starting a church. Many of these elements are basic and obvious. Yet many are all too often forgotten. We'll focus on three: having a burden for lost people, having a willingness to develop and participate in the vision, and having an ability to "sell" the vision to others.

A BURDEN FOR LOST PEOPLE

The church planter must have a Christlike burden for lost people. "Seeing the people, He [Jesus] felt compassion for them" (Matthew 9:36, NASB). Such must be the sincere attitude of the church planter.

Hundreds of church planters are at work across this country. Many diligently minister and relentlessly witness. Their burden for lost people compels them. They have no choice. Yet many other church planters labor diligently, not out of a burden for lost people, but because of their own drive for success, because of their own desire to pastor large churches, because of their own ambition. And while these church planters may reach some people along the way, eventually their misguided motivation will drive them away from church starting, perhaps even away from God.

The same misguided priorities exert control in the sponsoring of new churches. Many sponsoring churches in our country are driven by a burden for lost people. They sincerely embrace a kingdom vision, realizing there are people to be reached for Christ who may never come to their established church but may attend a new church. These established churches sacrificially give of themselves, expecting nothing in return except the satisfaction of knowing they are doing something to reach lost people for Christ.

Many other sponsoring churches, however, enthusiastically agree to help start new churches even though they have no burden for lost people. Their desire is for recognition from their peers. These churches do all they can to let others know of their works and to ensure that they get recognition. Yet soon the recognition dies down, and these churches find another pet project.

To develop a lasting vision for church planting, the church planter—and everybody else involved in starting a church, including the sponsoring church as well as the new church members—must have a concern for lost people. The cries of the city, the cries of the homeless, the cries of America must burden the church planter until he or she does something to reach these lost people for Christ.

A WILLINGNESS TO DEVELOP AND PARTICIPATE IN THE VISION

Next, the church planter must have, and be willing to participate in, a vision of what could be. The church planter must believe without hesitation that the lost people for whom he or she is burdened *can* be reached for Christ. As this vision begins to take shape, the church planter must yield to it. The church planter must move from having the vision to hearing the call to participate in that vision.

The church planter must also move from having the vision to developing the vision. The church planter should clarify or narrow the vision. In clarifying the vision, the church planter can ask, "What needs are present in this community? What need does this community have that nobody else is filling, or at least is not filling well?" Then the church planter can find a niche. He or she can find a way to become a valuable resource in the community.

Sometimes the need that is not being met in a community translates into groups that are not being ministered to. For example, churches may be neglecting senior adults, single adults, middle-aged adults, single parents, or the middle-income crowd. If there is a group in the community that is being overlooked by other local congregations, that may well be the cornerstone of the church vision.

One current phenomenon across the country is to build a church around the vision of reaching people who have turned their backs on traditional churches. There are enough people who have fallen through the cracks of traditional churches to fill up new churches all across the country. If the church planter can find common threads for these people, she or he can bring them into the church.

That is just one example of a vision that a church planter can develop and invest himself or herself in. God will show the way to those whom God has called for this purpose.

AN ABILITY TO "SELL" THE VISION

Last, the church planter must "sell" the vision, or persuade others to take it up as a cause. This begins with the church planter himself or herself becoming convinced that the vision *can* be realized, *must* be realized, and *will* be realized through Christ. The church planter must be certain that the new church can make a difference in the community. The church planter must be able to look someone in the eyes and say, "I need you, and you need this vision." And that person walks away saying, "I need to do this."

An Ability to "Sell" the Vision

How the church planter sells the vision depends on the personality of the church planter. However, this does not mean the church planter has to have a vibrant, slap-on-the-back, gregarious type of personality. Rather, the church planter must have a communicating personality, a listening personality, a people personality. The church planter must be serious and sincere about the vision and be able to communicate the vision to others.

The ability to communicate a vision comes as the church planter is properly prepared and knowledgeable about group-dynamic principles.

The Church Planter's Preparation

If the vision for a new church is to be transferred to other people, the church planter must be prepared. This preparation involves three crucial areas.

1. The church planter, much like a salesperson, must have full knowledge of the "product." The product, in this case, is the new church. The target audience for the new church, much like a consumer, will not know more than the salesperson about the product and what the product can or cannot do. Much of this knowledge grows out of the time the church planter has invested in studying the area and its needs.

2. The church planter must have full knowledge of the target audience. The church planter must know so much about the people to be reached—their strengths, weaknesses, and interests—that he or she can go into the community with a sense of confidence. Then the church planter can present the vision in such a way that the target audience will at least be open to hearing it.

3. The church planter must anticipate resistance to the vision. Every visionary meets resistance. But a visionary is able to look through the storm and see the sun. The visionary should expect objections and build the answers to those objections into the presentation of the vision. Often the visionary can answer questions before they are asked.

Group-Dynamic Principles

Furthermore, if the vision for a new church is to be transferred to others, the church planter must be familiar with group dynamics. Group dynamics dictate the following two principles.

1. The church planter should test the vision with one or two trusted people. As the church planter shares the vision with these people, they will bring an evaluation, analysis, or appraisal of the vision. These responses will help the church planter tighten the strategy or bring more clarity to the vision. And out of this process, the church planter will gain one or two allies. Then, with a more defined vision, the church planter can go on to still more people, who will also offer responses to the vision and become allies. And so on.

The most effective way to gain allies is to go to people personally. This gives individuals a personal stake in the vision and an opportunity to contribute something positive to it.

An Ability to "Sell" the Vision

Also, through this process, the church planter may bring together people who would not normally cooperate with each other. For example, person A may not ordinarily work in a positive way with person B. However, because each has been enlisted individually, they no longer see each other as adversaries but rather as teammates. Perhaps person A thinks person B has finally been convinced to see things the right way. And person B thinks the same about person A.

In short, personal enlistment enables the church planter to improve the vision, gain support, and bring people together.

2. The church planter should present the vision to the group of supporters. The church planter will have been developing and nurturing a loose collection of interested others through door-to-door campaigns, one-on-one conversations, and networking. The time comes when the church planter will need to present the vision to these people as a group in a more formal way. This presentation is for affirmation, for commitment, and most importantly, for a sense of ownership by the group.

In planning the presentation of the vision to the group, the church planter should take into consideration the fact that people receive information in a variety of ways. Some need to have information given to them through lectures or visual aids. Some receive it best in small groups where dialogue is possible, while others receive it best in a situation where they can reflect upon it over a longer period of time. Still others may best engage new information through some kind of hands-on interactive activity. And many get messages through some sort of musical presentation. A church planter should consider all these methods when developing a plan to sell the vision. Variety, like frequency, is key to a good vision-sharing strategy.

This presentation to the group is vital to the life of the vision. Sometimes church planters have begun to build a core group for a church but have neglected for too long to present their vision for starting a church from the group. Then, when the members of the core group hear the word "church" for the first time, they may run the other way.

For example, a church planter may begin with a home Bible study. And while in his or her mind this Bible study is the beginning of a potential church, the church planter says nothing about it to the Bible study attenders. When the church planter finally lets drop a mention of the church-planting vision, the Bible study members may say, "We just wanted a Bible study. We weren't looking for a church."

The opposite scenario can also occur. Some church planters, while building a core group, have shared the overall vision for starting a church but have failed to give a sense of the process or timing that will be followed. Therefore, some in the group have become eager to start the church immediately—before the right time has come. The church planter has to put on the brakes and regain control of the situation.

A part of sharing the vision in a group includes sharing as

many pieces of the game plan as possible along the way. The church planter thus gives the people a sense of the time and process involved in starting the church. A knowledge of group dynamics will enable a church planter to do this successfully.

CONCLUSION

Sometimes the obstacles to starting a new church seem insurmountable. Sometimes the church planter feels rejected. Nevertheless, the church planter cannot stop seeing or articulating the God-given vision for a new church in a predominantly black community. This takes perseverance and tenacity. It is not easy. But being true to the vision—and to the God who calls the church planter to that vision—is necessary to a journey in church planting.

CHAPTER 4

Understanding the Role of the Sponsoring Church

THE JOURNEY TO BEGIN A CHURCH IN A predominantly black community should not be made in isolation; it should be the result of a partnership. The most effective new works in any community are those that are done within the framework of a prayerful, committed relationship between a sponsoring church and a new church.

HELPFUL DEFINITIONS

Two definitions are helpful at this point. A *sponsoring church*—also known simply as a "sponsor"—is any congregation that has made a formal agreement to provide one or more resources for a specified period of time to help establish a viable, self-sufficient, autonomous body of believers. Resources may include money, facilities, teaching helps, leaders, or other things that would enable the new church to survive and to grow. A *new church*—also known as a "mission," "chapel," or "new work"—is a young congregation that has not yet reached the level of maturity or financial self-sufficiency to exist independently.

Often the sponsoring church/new church relationship is described in familial terms. The sponsoring church is the parent in the relationship. The new church is the child (usually known as the "daughter congregation") in the relationship. While such a description offers interesting analogies, it is generally inappropriate for describing a sponsor/mission relationship, especially when it is a cross-cultural sponsorship. Such sponsorships are inherently laden with issues of superiority and inferiority, independence and dependence. Any description or language that could bring these issues to the forefront, such as the parental model of sponsorship, should be avoided.

The relationship should be described in terms of a partnership. The sponsoring church and new church are partners in reaching people who have not yet been reached for Christ. The new church could not do this task on its own. Neither could the sponsoring church. Each needs the other.

Before looking closely at how one church sponsors another, let's look at why church sponsorship is not more common.

REASONS WHY CHURCHES DON'T SPONSOR

While a church can realize great dividends in the kingdom of God through the sponsorship of a new work, many healthy, strong churches that are able to sponsor new works are unwilling to do so. Here are a few reasons why established churches are unwilling to become sponsoring churches:

An Assumption That Others Will Take Responsibility

This is a dangerous attitude that seems almost hereditary within church families. A church that assumes some other church will take the responsibility in sponsoring a new work has little integrity when asking or expecting members to take responsibility in the church. Individual church members have made similar assumptions for years. "If I don't teach Sunday school, somebody else will." "If I don't give to the church, somebody else will." All church leaders know the error of individual church members in making these assumptions. It is similarly erroneous for churches to assume that another church body will fulfill their responsibility in starting new churches. More often than not, the responsibility goes unfulfilled, and God's plans are thwarted by a seemingly innocent assumption.

If this is what is holding a church back from sponsoring a new congregation, the solution is obvious: an attitude change is needed. Perhaps through a series of pastoral messages the church could be presented with the responsibility—and adventure—of contributing to God's mission in the world. Repentance and a turnaround of perspective would put such a church in a place where it could begin serving through new church sponsorship.

A Lack of Kingdom Values
Rather than an attitude that says, "We're all in this together," many churches develop an us-versus-everybody-else mentality. While such an isolationist attitude has occasional political attraction, it has no place in the church. It cannot be upheld scripturally.

Christians are first and foremost citizens of the kingdom of God rather than members of an individual church. Churches should invest at least as much effort into growing the kingdom of God as they do in growing their own churches.

How does growing the kingdom of God differ from growing a church? Essentially, *growing the kingdom of God* means that a church gives itself in ministering to, and sharing the Good News with, individuals who may never join their local church or make any kind of contribution to it. *Growing a church* means, once again, that the church gives itself in ministering to and sharing the Good News with individuals. But this time, the individuals are subtly expected to give something back to the church, usually in terms of becoming a member.

Sometimes a church understands the concept of a kingdom vision but refuses to accept it. This church becomes self-idolatrous. A church is so consumed with itself and its own preservation that it cannot see beyond itself. Such a self-absorption backfires and hurts the church that is trying so desperately to protect itself.

An Unwillingness to Pay the Price
Sponsoring a new church is costly—there's no denying it. What a sponsor gives will differ from situation to situation. However, a sponsoring church is often expected to give investments of money, time, and sometimes even church members as it helps establish a new church. Some churches are unwilling to sponsor a new church start because the price just looks too steep.

A sponsoring church must be willing to give of itself. Yet it need not be overly fearful. New churches are not given the "keys to the bank" of a sponsoring church. That is, new churches are not allowed to indiscriminately drain a church's financial and human resources for its own benefit. As a sponsoring church and a new church enter into a relationship, the two should sign a written agreement or covenant (discussed later in this chapter) outlining exact commitments of time, finances, and people between the two churches. Thus a sponsoring church will not become overburdened or overextended as it seeks to establish a new church.

A Fear of Diminishing Returns

Closely tied in to the unwillingness to pay the price is the fear that the sponsoring church will pay a great price in starting a church but will realize little in return, perhaps even experience a loss on its investment. This is an attitude in which the church mirrors societal trends and responses rather than basing its trends and responses upon Scripture.

Yet a church seriously involved in church starting must admit that the possibility of diminishing returns is real. Sometimes a sponsoring church expends much time, effort, and money in starting a new church that struggles along and never quite makes it on its own. So the fear of diminishing returns is not wholly without justification. Many times, the expectations of sponsoring church exceed the abilities of the planter and new congregation. The sponsoring leadership need to temper their expectations; the reality is that their efforts may produce a new church with substantially fewer members—and thus, fewer kingdom resources—than envisioned.

Although possible, diminishing returns are not probable. More often a sponsoring church is rewarded in seeing many people become Christians and involved in a local church. And even if the new church never becomes large, the small number of people it does reach are still of eternal value in the eyes of God. This fact reflects again the paradox of church planting being a necessary but often difficult journey.

No Vision for New Work

Many existing churches do not understand why new churches are needed. A prevalent belief is that there are enough existing churches to accommodate whoever wants to go to church. If an unchurched person were serious about wanting to go to church, then he or she could easily find an existing church to attend. Those with no vision for new work insist that, rather than putting resources into starting churches, Christians should put resources into strengthening existing churches. Impassioned and impressive arguments are made on this point.

Yet any twenty-first-century American—churched or unchurched—knows that people want choices. In fact, if one word could describe contemporary American culture, it would be *choice*. A simple trip to the grocery store confirms this. The sheer number of shampoos, cereals, and dog foods available can be overwhelming. If people have such choice and variety in these inconsequential matters, then they come to expect, and they deserve, choice and variety in churches.

One church simply cannot appeal to every person in a community. If a church seriously wants to reach its community for Christ, then it must realize that it cannot do it by itself. Some new churches must be started to reach specific cross sections of the community. To help start these new churches, existing churches must be willing first to give of themselves.

TRAITS OF A HEALTHY SPONSORING CHURCH

In describing the kind of congregation that would make a healthy sponsoring church, the most obvious step would be to turn around the reasons given for not starting churches. Thus a healthy sponsoring church would display the following characteristics.

1. Acceptance of responsibility in starting a church. The sponsoring church must believe that if it does not sponsor a church, then a church probably will not be sponsored and people will not be reached with the Good News.

2. Commitment to kingdom values. The sponsoring church must understand that it may not grow as a result of starting a church, but that the kingdom of God will grow.

3. Willingness to pay the price in finances, time, and church members. The sponsoring church must be willing to invest itself in the life of the new church.

4. Acceptance of the possibility of diminishing returns. Although diminishing returns are not the norm for sponsoring churches, the sponsoring church must be open to this risk. It must be ready to accept the possibility of not realizing immediate return on its investment.

5. Vision for new work. A healthy sponsoring church must have a vision for reaching its community. To do that, the existing church must be open to starting a variety of churches to reach the various people in its community.

Beyond these characteristics, a healthy sponsoring church exhibits several other traits that help make the relationship between sponsoring church and new church mutually satisfying. These traits include courage, selflessness, flexibility, and openness.

Courage

Starting a church is a step of faith. The sponsoring church must have courage to start a church in a community that may be totally different from the community in which it exists and among people who are different from its members.

Most church members are secure in a cocoon of likeness. They work, live, play, and go to church with people who are like them. To start a church among people of a different race, culture, socioeconomic status, or whatever takes tremendous courage. It mandates leaving the cocoon and entering the world.

The sponsoring church also must have courage to start a church in a community that, from all outward appearances, may already have enough churches. The sponsoring church may meet critics who question the need for another church. Many of these critics will even be brothers and sisters in the faith who fear a loss of members in their churches or unwanted competition from a new church in the community. The sponsoring church must have courage to meet these critics, not only with love, but also with hard data, proving why a new church is needed.

The sponsoring church also must have courage to invest its resources in what could be considered a risky venture. Many unknowns are inherent in starting a church. A sponsoring church must be willing to say, "Whatever the outcome, this church is going to invest itself in the life of this new church."

Selflessness

The sponsoring church must realize that in many ways it is giving itself away so that others might hear Christ's message. Starting a church means that the sponsoring church is putting its community first. It is thinking more of its community and the people who need to be reached than it is thinking of itself—its comfort, its bank account, its church rolls.

Flexibility

A sponsoring church must be flexible in its approach to starting a new church. An effective sponsoring church realizes that every situation is unique. What works in one situation may not work in another. What worked yesterday may not work today. The church that wishes to start another church is on the cutting edge of change and innovation. It must be ready to respond at a moment's notice when opportunities present themselves. It must be willing to change its methods of reaching people, if necessary, without changing its essential message. In doing so, it will be following the model established by Jesus when he was on the earth.

Openness

Closely tied to the trait of flexibility is the trait of openness. A sponsoring church must be open to new ideas and new ways of doing things. Because the new church does not have a history, it cannot say, "We never did it this way before." And because the sponsoring church wants to help the new church build a strong foundation for making its own history, it must not use those words either. The sponsoring church walks a fine line between using its years of experience and wisdom to offer helpful counsel to a new church and using its ingrained routines to force unnecessary conformity upon a new church. The sponsoring church should strive for the former and guard against the latter.

In addition, if the sponsoring church is from a different cultural background than that of the new church, the sponsoring church must be open to the value and worth of different cultural expressions of the gospel.

SPECIAL CHALLENGES OF CROSS-CULTURAL SPONSORSHIP

In many instances the sponsor of a new church in a predominantly black community will be a congregation with a different cultural background. Building a sponsoring church/new church relationship between churches of different cultural backgrounds presents many special challenges.

Special Challenges of Cross-Cultural Sponsorship

1. The sponsoring church and the new church should agree on the meaning of terms. For example, the term "resources" may mean money to one church and literature to another church. In building a cross-cultural relationship, one key is to never assume anything. Leaders of both the sponsoring church and the new plant should give as much attention as possible to details, definitions, and other tools to help build understanding.

2. The two churches should agree on the potential of the new church. Often individuals from different cultures would describe a "successful" church in different ways. For example, the sponsoring church may have a vision of the new church becoming a large, self-supporting church in a short period of time. However, if the new church is targeted to a small segment of the community occupying a low socioeconomic level, it may remain small and may require financial assistance for an extended period of time. Yet, though small and financially struggling, the new church could still be termed successful in that it is reaching people for Christ who otherwise would not be reached. In setting goals regarding the direction and future of the new church, both the sponsoring church and new church should be as precise and realistic as possible—clearly articulating expectations and consequent committments in the interest of realizing those expectations.

3. The two churches should respect differing styles of worship and spiritual expression. The history of African American Christians is directly tied to a unique worship style. A sponsoring church should not expect a new church to forgo years of cultural history and identity to please the sponsoring church. Likewise, a new church should not be critical or derisive if a sponsoring church worships God differently.

4. The two churches should respect differing church priorities. For example, black churches historically have had a strong commitment to Christian social ministry. In fact, *not* having a social ministry is not an option for these churches. Sponsoring churches should accept this priority, realizing that this new church, with its strong emphasis on practical ministry, is still a Bible-believing, gospel-preaching church.

5. The two churches should allow each other to explore relationships with other churches. For example, a black church may choose to enter into a fellowship with other black churches, some of which may not be a part of the sponsoring church's denomination. Rather than seeing this as a threat to its relationship with the new church, the sponsoring church should understand that such a fellowship speaks to needs that the sponsoring church may not be able to address. It offers a further environment within which the new church can grow and mature.

6. The two churches must build trust. Unfortunately, little trust exists among cultural groups in society today. At times, just when trust seems to be developing, something happens to upset the delicate balance. The challenge of building trust will require much time, prayer, perseverance, and honesty. Trust will not be built overnight. Trust will not be built without Spirit-led words and actions. Trust will not be built without the commitment to stick with it, despite the costs. Trust will not be built without some heart-wrenching, brutal honesty. And most importantly, churches will not be built without trust.

7. The two churches and their leaders must develop and understand expectations for each other. For example, the sponsoring church may expect the new church to provide written monthly reports regarding church activities, attendance, financial, and so forth matters. This could be seen as largely an Anglo expectation, because it is not a traditional process for the African American church. Thus, some black church leaders may view such an expectation as unnecessary and a nuisance. The two churches should agree upon expectations for their relationship and then strive to honor those expectations. The key is communication, understanding, and agreement.

GUIDELINES FOR SPONSORING CHURCH/NEW CHURCH RELATIONSHIPS

For a healthy, mutually satisfying relationship to develop between the sponsoring church and the new church, both parties should agree upon certain guidelines. And to prevent potential misunderstandings, these guidelines should be set forth in a covenant—a written document of agreement. The covenant should set forth the expectations and responsibilities of both the sponsoring church and the new church. As a foundation for this covenant, everyone involved in the process should understand that the new church is a part of the sponsoring church. Although the new church may meet in a different place and reach a different group of people, it still operates under the governance and authority of the sponsoring church until it becomes autonomous.

The sponsoring church and the new church should consider guidelines on such topics as church membership, the new pastor, equipment and property, the support committee, business meetings, church ordinances, finances, and the new church's eventual maturity.

Church Membership
Members of the new church are actually members of the sponsoring church. Therefore, those who desire membership in the mission must meet the membership requirements of the sponsoring church. The mission may receive members on behalf of the sponsoring church. Those joining the mission should join by one of these methods: (1) by baptism, after profession of faith; (2) by letter from another Baptist church; or (3) by a statement of faith and a statement of baptism. The clerk of the sponsoring church should maintain a membership list for the mission. The sponsoring church may also want to

make itself available to provide new member orientation and training classes for those who join the mission.

Members of any of the program organizations of the new church are also actually members of the corresponding program organizations of the sponsoring church. This may include Sunday school, discipleship training, women's ministry, men's ministry, and church music. The sponsoring church may want to provide leadership in establishing and developing any program organizations that the new church desires.

The New Church's Pastor

The new church and the sponsoring church should agree on the new church's pastor. A written document outlining principles, procedures, and guidelines for a joint pastor search committee could provide structure for this process. Even if the mission currently has a pastor, the document should be prepared so that it is available if needed in the future.

Just as with church members, the pastor of the new church is a member of the sponsoring church. Further, he is considered a staff member of the sponsoring church. The pastor of the new church and the pastor of the sponsoring church should develop a close relationship. The two should meet regularly to discuss goal setting, expectations, plans, activities, and evaluation. The pastor of the sponsoring church should prayerfully work with the pastor of the new church to help him or her develop vision, mission, and direction.

Equipment and Property

Equipment and property used by the new church should be maintained in the name of the sponsoring church until the mission is constituted as an autonomous church. At that time the equipment and property, along with any liabilities for the same, should be transferred to the new church.

The sponsoring church can provide a great service to the new church by emphasizing that the church is not a building but rather the people who meet there. It's not necessary to have a great meeting place or to own a building right from the start. But of course, a new church must have *someplace* to meet. And here there are lots of options to consider. The sponsoring church can help the new church look at alternative meeting places and the financial obligations they create.

The new church will want to pace itself and not overextend itself. At the time the new church is constituted, it should be able to maintain its location financially.

The Support Committee

The support committee represents the sponsoring church and should meet monthly with the mission pastor and one or more elected representatives from the mission. These meetings provide opportunity for reports, planning, and prayer for the mission. The support committee reports to the sponsoring church regarding the mission's needs and plans. This committee's task is to shepherd the vision of the new church, not to supervise or oversee the new church planter. These persons facilitate the new church by leveraging their influence on behalf of the vision of the new church plant.

Business Meetings

The mission should hold regular business meetings to discuss and vote on matters of business, which will then be given to the sponsoring church for approval. These business meetings should include nomination and election of officers and leaders for the mission.

Church Ordinances

The observances of the church ordinances—baptism and the Lord's Supper—should be conducted in accordance with the sponsoring church's constitution or approval. The mission pastor and sponsoring church pastor should work together in planning observances of the ordinances.

Finances

The mission should submit a recommended budget to the support committee, which in turn will recommend it to the sponsoring church for approval. Some stipulation should be agreed upon regarding nonbudget expenditures that would require the sponsoring church's approval. Monthly mission financial reports should be provided to the support committee, although, as mentioned above (see Cross-Cultural Challenges), this expectation should be clearly articulated between the sponsoring and newly planted church leadership.

The mission should give a definite percentage of its tithes and offerings to its denomination to support missions. (And it should plan to increase this percentage in the future.) Additionally, the mission should give a definite percentage of its tithes and offerings to support other new church plants.

The mission and sponsoring church should have a written understanding regarding the amount and duration of financial assistance the sponsoring church will provide. Any stipulations regarding how the funds are to be used should also be agreed upon in writing. For example, the sponsoring church may provide funds specifically for facility rental; purchase of a building or property; construction of a building; the pastor's salary, housing, and retirement; or purchase of curriculum, hymnals, and promotional materials.

When the mission is constituted as a separate church, all funds and liabilities become the property of the new church.

The Maturity of the New Church

When a congregation has become mature enough to govern itself and to be financially self-supporting, preparation should be made to constitute the mission into a self-governing church. There is no set timetable as to when this should occur. However, this should be a part of the strategic plan for the new church plant. And normally it should occur within a five- to seven-year time frame.

Regrettably, some missions—because of their location, constituency, or any number of other reasons—believe they may never be able to constitute into an autonomous church. They might even begin to think of themselves, not as a new church plant, but as an ongoing ministry of the sponsoring church. An important distinction between a ministry opportunity and a new church is the ability of the mission to eventually handle its own finances and call its own pastor.

The sponsoring church should be prepared to face these cases by carefully designing and monitoring the progress of the plan of the new church. This plan should take into consideration the economic strengths of the target community. For example, it is foolhardy to put a full-time church planter in a community that is economically disadvantaged and cannot support the full-time planter. In this case a bivocational church planter or even a lay church planter is the better option to pursue. An alternative like this would not lay such a heavy financial burden on the new church that it would kill the energy needed to be successful. These alternatives should not be viewed as inferior choices. They reflect an understanding of contextually driven strategy development.

CONCLUSION

To be a sponsoring church is a privilege. It offers a church a unique opportunity to become a partner with other believers in reaching people for Christ. It often pumps new life into an otherwise comfortable and sometimes lethargic congregation.

To be a sponsoring church is also an awesome responsibility and challenge. It demands the selfless giving of valuable resources. Further, cross-cultural sponsorships demand the breaking down of stereotypes between cultural groups and the hammering out of renewed relationships built on respect and acceptance.

Regrettably, many churches look no further than the staggering responsibility when determining whether sponsoring a new congregation is for them. They give church starting only a fleeting thought, afterward turning their thoughts and energies inward. As in churches where the minority of church members do the vast majority of church work, so these self-centered churches happily allow a committed minority of churches to do the majority of church starting. In so doing, they miss out on one of the most invigorating and rewarding ventures possible—bringing countless individuals into a saving relationship with Christ and into a local body of believers.

CHAPTER 5

Understanding the Role of the New Church Pastor

AS JESUS JOURNEYED TOWARD THE LAND OF the Samaritans, so we must continue our journey to lands unknown. We cannot go as a loosely aligned group of people with varying abilities, interests, motivations, and commitments. If we were to do so, our journey would become no more than random wanderings. Rather, we must continue our journey purposefully. And if we are to do this, a leader must emerge. This leader will be able to mold our motley band of believers into a unified, visionary group. This leader is the pastor.

At first glance, it may seem obvious that a pastor is necessary to a church-starting venture. However, some may argue that, if we believe in the priesthood of the believer, then we should not emphasize the pastor's role in church starting. If all believers are on an equal plane in the sight of God, and if all are rightfully seen as ministers, then cannot a group of committed, visionary laypersons start a church as well as a pastor can? The answer is yes and no.

Stories abound of groups of lay believers who became burdened about their communities and began meeting in homes for prayer and Bible study. Soon these spontaneous prayer meetings gave birth to churches and, somewhere along the way, pastors were called to assume leadership of these self-started congregations.

Our point is that such pastors are necessary to the continued growth and vitality of new churches. Although any believer who is connected with a new church is vital and has a specific role to fulfill as a minister of the gospel, the pastor is indispensable. Without a pastor convinced that a new church is needed and committed to giving whatever it takes to start that church, a new church will falter and probably fail. The pastor provides vision and leadership for the congregation and offers a worthy model of perseverance when circumstances are discouraging.

Not just any pastor will do, however. Church starting in the black community takes the *right* pastor. The choice of pastor "usually is the most important decision in launching a new congregation," says church growth specialist Lyle Schaller. He explains, "Frequently, the identity of that new church is a reflection of the personality, gifts, gender, values, experience, nationality, race, education, priorities, family status, political views, theological stance, social class, age, and hobbies of the pastor."[1]

The prominence of the pastor in the black church tradition is even more pronounced than in the white church tradition. "The central figure in the Black Church is the black preacher," C. Eric Lincoln says unequivocally. "The black preacher includes a dimension peculiar to the black experience."[2]

That peculiar dimension can be likened to the historical role of the black tribal chieftain—a leader who influenced others not only religiously but also socially, culturally, and politically. Lincoln describes the black pastor as a "projection of the people themselves."[3] That historical tradition lives on today, even for younger blacks who have little or no church experience.

Black pastors are spiritual leaders, but they are also much more. That's why selecting the right pastor is so important.

WHO THE RIGHT PASTOR *IS NOT*

Who is the right pastor for a new church in a predominantly black community? To answer that question, let us first examine who *is not* the right pastor.

Pastor Default

The right pastor to start a church in a black community is not one who accepts the responsibility by default. We will refer to this person as Pastor Default. First, Pastor Default says one of two things: "I don't see a church out there that I want" or "No church has called me." Pastor Default then says, "So, at least for now, I'll try this: I'll start a church. If it doesn't work out, surely something else will come along eventually." In the absence of other pastoral opportunities, Pastor Default reluctantly accepts a church-starting assignment. Pastor Default has an attitude problem, and that poor attitude would be translated into an unsatisfactory church-starting experience.

Pastor Black

The right pastor to start a church in the black community is also not just anybody who is black. We will refer to this person as Pastor Black. The color of Pastor Black's skin becomes the sole criterion for determining whether this person is the right pastor for the new church. No consideration is given to other significant factors, such as Pastor Black's theology or ability to relate to people or to identify with the community.

One historical example demonstrating that all blacks are not the same occurred in the late 1950s when a large number of blacks were migrating from the South to the North. Those who went north did not merge into the existing black churches; instead, they started their own. The reason was simple. Blacks from the South were socially and culturally different from northern blacks. If you were a black from Jackson, Mississippi, you were different in many ways from a black born and raised in Chicago, Illinois. Other factors, equally as important as race, determined whether a person was comfortable in a community. Even today, some churches in the North have "state" clubs, such as the Mississippi Club, for church members from that particular state.

A person's race is important, but it certainly is not the only factor that should be considered in selecting the right pastor for a new church. With a lack of consideration regarding the whole person selected as pastor, both the new church and the pastor could be entering into a precarious relationship.

Pastor Education

Furthermore, the right pastor to start a church in a black community is not necessarily the person with the most educational degrees. We will refer to this person as Pastor Education. An obvious tendency for a sponsoring church is to consider only those candidates who have specific educational qualifications. After the rudimentary educational requirements imposed on candidates by the sponsoring church, those candidates with additional educational qualifications are viewed as superior.

As with the consideration of a person's race, education is an important factor in selecting a pastor, but it is certainly not the only one. Sometimes quality individuals are summarily dismissed as potential candidates simply because they do not meet the educational requirements. Rather than upholding a rigid set of standards, a sponsoring church would do well to exercise sensitivity and openness to the Holy Spirit in matching the person with the context.

Two current trends support such fluidity. One trend is for people to leave their careers and respond to calls to the ministry. Such individuals may easily attain the necessary educational qualifications even while they are in the ministry. A second trend is for missions to begin looking for a pastor or spiritual leader from within the congregation rather than from elsewhere. Such a pastor would already have the necessary vision and commitment that someone from outside the community of believers might not have.

WHO THE RIGHT PASTOR *IS*

If neither Pastor Default, nor Pastor Black, nor Pastor Education is the right leader for the new church, then who is? A sponsoring church should consider several factors in identifying a pastor for a new church plant. None of these is race-specific; they are universal principles critical to the process of starting a church in any community. But they must be applied to each specific situation. Among these factors are the following: compatibility, accountability, vision, knowledge, risk taking, sociability, and commitment.

Compatibility

The candidate and the community in which the new church is to be located must be compatible. The two must be matched economically and socially as much as possible.

People may argue convincingly for heterogeneity in a church's makeup. However, the reality is that people tend to gravitate toward those like themselves. The more the new pastor becomes ingrained into the community, the more likely the church is to reach people for Christ. For example, some pastors would work well in the inner city but would feel ill at ease in the suburbs, while others would be at home in the suburbs and would be totally out of place in the inner city. If someone is out of context socially and economically when entering a new church community, it stands to reason that the relationship between the church and pastor would be potentially troublesome.

The key here is that the leaders of the church plant must study the target community thoroughly before selecting a pastor for the new church. They must take into account the complexity of the black community when selecting a pastor. Making broad generalizations or assumptions about a community just because its primary racial makeup is black is a serious error that could result in difficulties for the new church and the pastor.

The new pastor must be able to exhibit adaptability, compatibility, and flexibility in relating to the surrounding neighborhood. Likewise, community residents, and particularly new church members, must show an openness and respect toward the new pastor.

Accountability

The candidate and the sponsoring church must have a mutual understanding and commitment to their covenant relationship. The sponsoring church must make an effort to explain the covenant relationship with the candidate. All involved need to understand what to expect from each other. This kind of understanding should be ironed out before the first dollar, the first acre of land, or the first anything is committed.

If such understandings are not worked out, the church planter may have a distorted understanding of accountability. Thus, when the sponsoring church requires a report or some other indicator of accountability, the church planter may cry foul and accuse the sponsoring church of paternalism. Unfortunately, *paternalism* has become a catchword often misapplied to what is actually accountability.

The new church pastor should understand that members of the new church are technically members of the sponsoring church. That concept extends to the pastor, who is actually a staff member of the sponsoring church. When the pastor sees the relationship in that perspective, he or she is more likely to understand personal accountability to the sponsoring church. The sponsoring church has a right and an obligation to know what is going on in the new church.

New churches in black communities, sponsored by predominantly white churches, seem to have a bigger problem with this issue than do churches in black communities sponsored by other black churches. Black church leaders and members have come to expect an attitude of paternalism from their white counterparts, so when anything even resembling accountability occurs, charges of paternalism are raised. This is especially true among black Christians who have not had a lot of experience in working with whites. However, the problem also occurs in black churches sponsored by other black churches. The most effective deterrent to this problem is for both the new church pastor and the sponsoring church to have a clear understanding regarding the terms of the relationship before anything is formalized.

Vision

The new church pastor must have a holistic vision of planting churches. As sponsoring churches interview potential candidates for the new church pastorate, questions need to be raised about each candidate's vision of the ministry of church planting. Ideally, the new church pastor should have an attitude that says, "Not only do I want to plant a church but also I want to plant a church that will plant a church." In other words, the pastor should articulate a desire not only to become the pastor of a great church within one context but also to help in reaching lost people in other contexts.

Why is it important that the new church pastor articulate

that type of vision? There are several reasons. First, the pastor has been the recipient of such a vision on the part of the sponsoring church and should be able to give to others what she or he has received. Second, enlisting new church pastors with a kingdom vision helps to build an army of people committed to starting churches where there are lost people. Nothing less than such an army will come close to accomplishing the church-planting task. Third, the pastor with a kingdom vision for starting churches will be able to weather the storms that most certainly will come in the church-starting venture. Those with a broader vision are better equipped to handle minor setbacks and crises than are those who can only see the here and now.

Knowledge

The new church pastor must be willing to diligently study the community in order to determine the kind of church the community needs. The new church pastor should have a finger on the pulse of the community where the church is to be planted, because it is from this sort of intimate knowledge that a specific church-starting strategy can be developed. Too often, a church-planting strategy has been the exact opposite. A strategy has exhibited nothing new and has not been community-specific. The attitude could be expressed like this: "I'm just going to put up a building and open up for business on Sundays." That kind of strategy will go nowhere in the black community.

The new church pastor must first look at the demographic information available on the area and its residents. Such information might include data on income level, family makeup, educational background, type of housing, age, male-female ratios, and number of children. The local denominational leader usually has access to much of this information. The role of the sponsoring church is to help the new church pastor interpret this data accurately.

Demographic information is necessary and helpful. But while it answers many questions, it is not enough. The new church pastor must also acquire information about the community that cannot be read on a page. The pastor must be willing to walk with the community residents, to listen to them, to learn from them. The pastor must be able to articulate and to care about and indeed to be consumed by the needs of the community. The pastor must be able to answer the question of why another church is needed in that particular community.

The most successful new churches target the most critical needs in the community. One example of targeting critical needs can be seen in a mission of Southwest Community Baptist Church in Houston, Texas. A critical need in the community was to minister to children with sickle-cell anemia who, because of their illness, were forced to miss school frequently. The new church plant began a ministry which uses volunteers to tutor these children in their homes when they are absent from school.

Jesus is our model in sensitively addressing needs. He knew the people to whom he was ministering, to whom he was presenting the gospel. And he tailored his message to fit their needs. The new church pastor must do the same.

The new church pastor should also understand that, as the church is planted, the vision or strategy for the church may not be complete. And it probably will not be complete for some time. The people who respond to the church in its early years will do a lot to create and develop the personality of the church.

The contemporary terminology for this approach is "market segmentation." It is a valid concept for church planting because it can indicate what the target community needs and wants from a new church. From the type of ministries needed to the style of worship desired, all can be ascertained from this type of research.

Risk Taking

The new pastor must be bold—a risk taker. Starting a church, especially a church designed to meet community needs, is risky business. One runs the risk of being misunderstood, of being seen as competition from existing churches, of being ignored. It is not as big a risk for the new church pastor to start a church that is a duplicate of what every other church looks like. But it is a large risk to start a church that offers something new, established upon the lines of a new model for church. And that's exactly the kind of church that is destined to be most successful in reaching people. The new church pastor must be willing to lead the church in daring to minister in the community even though it is safer to stay inside the four walls of the church.

How willing is the new church pastor to take risks? Does the new church pastor see risks as problems or as opportunities? How creative is the pastor in developing a church relevant for today's society?

Sociability

The new pastor must like people. He or she must want to spend time with people and get involved in their lives.

This characteristic for the new church pastor may seem trite. It may seem so obvious that it does not need to be stated. Unfortunately, that is not always the case. Good and sincere people have entered the ministry, only for it to soon become obvious that they did not care deeply about other people. Their ministries were doomed to failure.

A sponsoring church should always try to ensure that a new church pastor exudes Christ's love and concern for others.

Commitment

The new church pastor must make a tremendous commitment to the church-starting task. Church starting is not a casual undertaking. It is not for the fainthearted or the easily discouraged. The new church pastor must have a burning passion for new work. Indeed, the pastor must make a commitment to the task that is similar to the commitment a foreign missionary would make—to go in and fulfill God's calling, in spite of the odds.

A new church pastor must yield to the call God has given, to the commitment God requires, to the passion Jesus demands of those who are going to love God's people.

CONCLUSION

As our journey—the journey of church starting in black communities—continues, the new church pastor must affirm that the black community does not need any more mediocre churches. It needs churches that will make a difference. New church pastors must be the sort of people who dedicate themselves to making that affirmation a reality.

Notes
1. Lyle E. Schaller, Forty-Four Questions for Church Planters *(Nashville: Abingdon, 1991), 108.*
2. C. Eric Lincoln, ed., The Black Experience in Religion *(Garden City, N.Y.: Anchor, 1974), 65.*
3. Ibid., 67.

CHAPTER 6

Steering a Course through the Obstacles

THE TWISTS AND TURNS AND UPS AND DOWNS OF OUR journey become increasingly evident the further we travel. These are the obstacles to starting and growing churches in predominantly black communities. Although disheartening, they do not have to be life-threatening. Although seemingly ever-present, they need not become our traveling companions.

Those involved in starting and growing churches in predominantly black communities may encounter several common obstacles. These include an overemphasis on numerical growth, selfishness among churches and denominations, a hesitation to let black churches set their own course, the temptation to talk about social issues without doing anything about them, a tendency to avoid sponsorship, and a failure to adapt to the circumstances of modern society. In this chapter we will look at each of these obstacles, the hope being that as a result churches and church leaders will be better prepared to steer safely around each obstacle as it appears in their path.

THE NUMBERS GAME

"The bottom line." "Risk management." These are some of today's buzzwords. They reflect the numbers game of counting people and dollars. But can such concepts apply to our church-starting task? In a sense, they cannot apply. In another sense, they must.

Numbers come into play in at least two areas in church starting: choosing the location of a new church and gauging a new church's success.

Where Is a New Church Needed?

How does one determine where a new church is needed? More than one source of information can help in making this critical decision.

For one thing, those involved in church planting must consider demographics and statistics. Church-to-population ratios present telling evidence about the need for new churches. These numbers provide solid, objective information—the type of information that leaders must consider in order to make difficult decisions about where to place resources. These leaders are more likely to respond when the need is obvious.

Yet objective information is not the only consideration in determining where to start a church. A certain subjectivity must be allowed. Often God leads an individual to sense needs and to feel burdened to meet those needs, even though the burden may not match up with the results of a statistical needs assessment. This subjectivity cannot be quantified or packaged. Neither can it be denied.

Generally, denominational decision makers have been more inclined toward considering quantifiable data in determining where a new church is needed. Because these people are not on the mission field where needs are obvious, this is a method of research they can rely on.

Meanwhile, those in the hands-on ministry have been more inclined toward the subjective realization of a need. They do not have the luxury of cross tabulations showing where churches and people are located.

To determine the need for churches in black communities, neither approach should be used exclusively. Indeed, using one to the exclusion of the other is a trap that could mean some desperately needed churches are not started. Both approaches are valuable if used correctly.

Numbers can help us to become more attuned to the leadership of God's Holy Spirit, but they have also been used to squelch that leadership. Those with the authority to make decisions about where to plant churches must not allow statistics to undermine God's leadership of individuals.

Conversely, while those who realize a need through prayer and communion with God can proclaim God's desires more clearly than anyone, those same individuals have at times doggedly denied that God could lead through statistics or speak to denominational decision makers. Potential church planters should not negate the tremendous tool of statistical, marketing, and demographic information that God provides.

Determining where a new church is needed is a both/and proposition. God leads objectively through statistics, marketing, and demographics. God also leads subjectively through individuals sensing a burden.

A good example of how God can lead both subjectively and objectively is that presented by Brentwood Baptist Church in Houston, Texas, where Joe Ratliff serves as pastor. In 1965, when an existing church was considering the start and sponsorship of Brentwood, statistics supported the new church start, but only in a limited way. The numbers revealed that people were moving to this bedroom community. Statistics further indicated the new church would be a community church, with a maximum membership of eight hundred people. In addition, deed restrictions placed the new church in an area of low visibility and relative inaccessibility—two factors that could mean trouble for any new church.

However, nothing in the statistics foreshadowed the impact Brentwood would have on its entire city. Because of the vision of its leaders and the undeniable involvement of the Holy Spirit, Brentwood is now a regional church with a membership in the thousands. The average church member drives fifteen miles to church. Brentwood has itself started fourteen churches in its thirty-six year history, all of them sponsored during Ratliff's twenty-plus years in the pastorate. That statistic reflects his visionary leadership and commitment to new church planting.

We can learn from examples like that one that numbers must not be used to undermine the work of the Holy Spirit. We must listen to numbers and pay attention to statistics and other good information, but at the same time we must realize that God can transcend numbers.

Is the New Church Successful?

How does one determine the success of a new church? Once again, numbers must be considered but are not the sole, nor perhaps even the best, consideration in determining the success of the new church. Using numbers to measure the success of a venture is, by and large, the secular approach that Christians have bought in to. "Bigger is better," the motto goes. The emergence of the megachurch in the 1980s and 1990s may seem to lend credence to this belief. But for every megachurch there are two hundred smaller churches.

Which church is more successful: a suburban church that averages thousands of worshipers each Sunday morning and has the budget to air its worship services on television, or an inner-city church that struggles to have thirty-five attend on a Sunday morning and still receives a stipend from its sponsoring church after seven years? The answer is "none of the above." Neither church is more successful than the other. Or rather, each church is successful as it is being faithful to God in following the Great Commission.

Unfortunately, those of us involved in church starting, in an attempt to challenge a church to grow and to become self-supporting, often impose debilitating standards upon it. If a church does not have the numbers or the financial resources to have a full-time pastor, staff, and all of those other things that we want for our churches, then that church may mistakenly be labeled a failure. And in all probability the church will then live up to that label.

What exactly do we want for our churches? As we answer that question, we find that what we want for our churches is greatly influenced by our mentors, past experiences, former pastorates, degree of self-confidence, faith in people around us, and other factors. In short, what we want is largely a product of our environment. Most church leaders agree on the substance of a new church start. When we start talking about form, however, is when we differ and start assigning labels to ourselves and others.

We must realize that not all churches will reach large numbers of people, have full-time pastors or staff, or even become self-supporting within our preferred time frame. But that is acceptable, because not all churches are alike.

At the same time we must affirm that churches should be challenged to grow and to become all that God intends for them to be. Churches should be encouraged to set growth goals. Churches should be undergirded with support and affirmation so that they are able to do ministry and grow spiritually and perhaps numerically.

A church's success is measured through tangibles—number of church members, size of budget, and the like. A church's success is also measured through intangibles—an individual with a changed life, a ministry to the forgotten.

Looking Out for Number One

Looking out for number one—that is, becoming egocentric—is a common obstacle faced not only by new churches in black communities but also by the denominations starting them. Secular values press in on churches and denominations, compelling them to pattern themselves after society rather than to model themselves upon Christ's example.

New churches struggle to establish their identities, to raise budgets, perhaps to build facilities. New churches also face the skepticism and outright negativism of other churches (and perhaps from other denominations) active in their communities. All of these reasons tempt churches to turn inward, keeping their resources and plans to themselves, even though their purpose is to reach outward into the communities.

While churches are wrestling with these challenges, entire denominations are doing the same. Predominantly white denominations often have a history of questionable involvement in the black community, and that history seems to sabotage today's best efforts at starting churches in predominantly black communities. Skepticism and negativism on the local level are compounded immeasurably on the national level. As denominations question the motives of other denominations, the tendency is to turn inward, to take a we-don't-need-them attitude.

What is the answer to these challenges for churches and denominations? First, let's acknowledge that American Baptist and Southern Baptist proposals for church starting in predominantly black communities are aggressive. This aggressiveness comes with what some would call arrogance. But perhaps *confidence* is a more appropriate term than *arrogance*.

This confidence must be kept in perspective. It must be a confidence in Christ—that is, a confidence in what he has called us to do and in the power he provides—rather than self-confidence. Also, while acknowledging the sometimes negative history of white Baptists in the black community, we must confidently rise above it. We must patiently remind our critics, "That was then; this is now."

The second answer to the challenges of egotism is to develop a kingdom vision. Churches must resist the tendency to turn inward. They must strive to be a part of their denomination—all the way from the local judicatory to the state, regional, and national levels. This may mean sacrifice in terms of time and money. It may also mean some skepticism from your own folk (which is more difficult to take than suspicions from strangers). In the end, the benefits of being part of a larger family will outweigh the costs.

Churches must also strive to become part of the larger religious community—the very community that is not so sure you should be starting churches. While acknowledging that we feel called to serve God in this way at this time, we must also acknowledge that other churches and denominations have stakes in black communities as well. Denominations that want to start congregations in black communities must be willing to be partners in winning a community to Christ, and they must take an honest, nonpaternalistic approach toward those who are already in the black community and doing a good job. Denominations must be willing to say, "What can we do together to reach this community for Christ? What can we learn from each other?"

As church leaders become acquainted, share each other's burdens, and pray together, something good may happen. A cohesiveness can develop. Suspicions may dissolve. People will be reached—and it won't really matter who reaches them. With this kind of effort, we can transform entire cities and our nation. But it means working together as churches and denomination over the long haul.

While it is natural and necessary to look out for ourselves, we must not do so to the exclusion of others.

Plotting Our Own Futures

A major point of tension between a new congregation and a sponsoring church is that of the sponsoring church's allowing the new congregation to be itself rather a clone of the sponsoring church. This tension has caused many relationships to break down and others to never begin. It is a serious obstacle. What is the answer?

At least two points are important to remember here. First, it is the role of the sponsoring church to educate the new congregation on what it means to be a part of the larger Christian community and a denominational family. Second, the sponsoring church must allow the new congregation to (in a sense) chart its own destiny.

When a sponsorship is done right, the two congregations will share many commonalties. However, they will also have many differences.

An example of this similar-but-different condition comes from Faith Community Baptist Church, which Michael Cox helped to plant in 1984. In this new congregation's budget appeared the traditional Southern Baptist items, such as Cooperative Program and associational missions. But one item in the budget differed greatly from anything the sponsoring church had ever had in its budget: a contribution to the United Negro College Fund. When the sponsoring church reviewed the budget, this contribution was immediately questioned. After an open conversation about how the new congregation felt a keen commitment to education in the black community and how the contribution helped to meet that commitment, the sponsoring church responded affirmatively. That's the way it should be.

But there are many issues that may arise in the relationship, and each one must be handled carefully.

Worship Styles

One possible area of tension or misunderstanding between a sponsoring church and a new church is worship style. For example, if the sponsoring church is an Anglo church with a traditional Anglo worship service, and if it expects the new church it is sponsoring in a black community to worship in the same way, it is likely to get some resistance. And conversely, the black church might have some criticism for the style of worship practiced by its sponsoring Anglo congregation.

Rather than insisting that the worship style of the new church emulate that of the sponsoring church, both churches should allow worship to emanate from the cultures of the communities within which those churches are planted. The principle is this: true worship emanates rather than emulates.

Traditional black worship has certain characteristics. It is highly participatory, features quality music, is spontaneous, and emphasizes preaching. A new church start should be permitted to reflect the black worship tradition, if it wishes, regardless of how the sponsoring church worships. And at the same time the mission should consider itself free to modify the black worship tradition to be even more appropriate for the community of which it is a part, making its worship style truly its own.

Replication Tension

As issues like differences in worship reveal, the tendency for many sponsoring churches is to look upon the new congregation as a "baby." As the sponsoring church nurtures that new church, the desire grows to try to make the new church resemble its sponsoring church in every way. This is a mistake.

Just as parents need to let their children develop according to the way God has made them, so the new church should be allowed to grow naturally and become what God means for it to become. During this growth process, however, the sponsoring church should provide much-needed guidance and support.

There may be much give-and-take between a new congregation and its sponsoring church. There may be disagreements. There may be lengthy discussions and explanations. In the end, however, the sponsoring church should accept the new congregation's personality and grant it some measure of freedom to develop that personality.

The denominational structure must also allow churches in black communities to be themselves. In particular, churches in black communities cannot be expected to emulate the qualities and actions of white churches. The cookie-cutter mentality that says "You must look like me, act like me, and walk like me" will not work as traditionally white denominations step into black communities.

REHEARSING OR REVERSING?

Another common obstacle faced by a new church in the black community is the decision about how deeply to become involved in social and justice issues.

Most ministers in these churches are not reluctant to preach from the pulpit about the inhumanity or injustice of certain situations or issues. Church members encourage and expect such forthright preaching. But without accompanying actions, the words become empty—a simple rehearsal of the issues rather than a reversal of actual conditions.

Throughout history the black church has vigorously seized the role of social activist. It has identified and worked to deal with community needs, issues, and problems. The black church has presented Jesus Christ not only as our eternal Savior but also as our contemporary Redeemer. The cause of Christ inspired the church to be outspoken and involved. At these times the black church has been at its best. It earned the attention and respect of the whole community because it initiated or activated positive social change.

As churches are started in black communities across our country today, each must examine its reason for being and its role in the community. New churches in black communities should be designed from their births with the intention of not just rehearsing negative social realities from their pulpits and halls but of reversing those realities by getting involved in their communities. Churches designed with that purpose or scope develop a compelling presence in their communities and exhibit a magnetism for community residents.

GOING IT ALONE

For some new churches in black communities, the sponsoring church/new church relationship can become an obstacle. Though this relationship was originally intended as a help to the church plant, it comes to be viewed as a hindrance.

Fear, uncertainty, pride, and distrust may combine to influence a new congregation to go it alone, that is, to reject sponsoring-church assistance. And the sponsoring church may not question the rejection, because it is experiencing some of the same negative feelings about the relationship. Thus "sponsorship" becomes sponsorship on paper only. The full richness of the relationship is never tapped. When this happens, much is lost. Much pain and struggle that could have been avoided are borne.

One reason for the negative feelings that may arise in connection with sponsorship comes from history. Traditionally, black churches have not started other churches with the kind of direct support that denominations are offering today. Rather, black churches have been started with only the limited resources of those who have chosen to affiliate with the new congregation. And so, while churches in black communities could certainly find uses for the wealth of resources offered by denominations, they are not sure why the denominations are supposedly being so openhanded with this long-ignored group. Churches in black communities also want to resist the temptation to become affiliated with any denomination because of the lure of abundant resources.

A reason why potential sponsoring churches harbor such negative feelings has to do with the challenge of cross-cultural sponsorship. White churches have little, if any, experience in black communities. They don't understand the black worship experience. When faced with even moderate resistance from black church starters, white church members too easily declare, "Fine. If they want to do it on their own, we'll let them."

The solution to overcoming this obstacle is not simple. It will take models of how a sponsoring church and a new congregation can link hearts and hands to reach a community for Christ. It needs people who are willing to try this approach and let others know about their successes and failures.

One approach to a solution could be linking new congregations with prayer sponsors. The two congregations could hold prayer meetings about new work, praying specifically for the new church members. Thus prayer would become the link between the congregations. Although the two groups of people may pray differently, prayer (while, of course, primarily being communication with God) will have a therapeutic effect on the ones praying. Using prayer as a focal point could do much to steer clear of this obstacle and to develop the new work.

THINKING ABOUT TOMORROW

Many churches today are caught in a sort of time warp that causes them to be many years behind current trends. Most church planters smugly nod their heads in agreement. *It's a shame that established churches are not more open to new outlooks,* they think.

But being in a time warp is not limited to established churches; new churches suffer from the same problem. And thus here is another obstacle they face.

Starting new churches is not supposed to be an exercise in putting new wine into old wineskins (Matthew 9:17). In other words, church planters should not be creating a new church that's just as old-fashioned as some church that's been around for decades. But people are guilty of doing it anyway. It gives them what's familiar and comfortable. It affirms their mental model of church.

The fear of failure will drive people to put together in a

new church what was successful in the past. The problem is they do not take into consideration the full context of the new opportunity. They simply try to duplicate their past mental models of church in a new era with new people. That is a mistake, albeit a normal and understandable one. It should be avoided.

Church starters who try to institute traditional church life are often the ones whose churches struggle and stay mediocre. These are the church planters who try to implement status quo patterns and reconstruct previous experiences in new contexts. They are, in effect, inflexible and insensitive to the people they are trying to reach.

Nowhere in America are trends changing at a more mind-boggling pace than in the area of race and ethnicity. For example, in 1860 there were three census categories for race; in the latest census there were thirty categories. More and more Americans are proudly identifying themselves on the basis of a mixed heritage. And while these Americans are in many ways adapting American culture, they want to continue their understanding and practice of customs peculiar to their cultures.

Church planters who understand America's rapid racial changes and dare to speak to these changes in a positive, affirming, and different voice are often the ones whose churches are really making a difference. These church planters adapt tradition and adopt patterns to accommodate today's, not yesterday's, unchurched. They are flexible in allowing the new church's programs, worship times, ministries, and activities to reflect the needs of those whom they are trying to reach. In effect, these church planters are saying to the unchurched, "We want you badly enough to do whatever it takes, with the exception of changing our message, to reach you."

To avoid the temptation to do church as it has always been done, a new church must seize the opportunity to create and mold its own life. The new church must resist being a replication of what has been. It must be willing to struggle and discover its purpose and possibilities. The church in the black community is generally open to the idea of innovation, of not being wed to tradition. But to make this concept work, the new church needs support from its sponsoring church.

The sponsoring church must embrace this concept of not doing business as usual. It must challenge the new church to do things differently, to be sensitive to the community and God's Word, to discover why God wants the new church in that particular community. In this way it will help the new church overcome a serious obstacle.

CONCLUSION

In the course of this book, no promises have been made that starting churches in black communities is easy or stress-free. It takes effort, hard work, prayer, flexibility, perseverance, openness, commitment.... The list goes on. It may not be easy, but God's leadership is evident in this undertaking, and God will provide all that is needed.

In starting churches in black communities, be prepared to face the obstacles outlined in this chapter (and perhaps others). And as you face these obstacles, work through them. Do not let them detour you from your journey. Look upon these obstacles as opportunities to grow and to be stretched by God and others.

BIBLIOGRAPHY

Ahlen, J. Timothy, and J. V. Thomas. *One Church, Many Congregations: The Key Church Strategy* (Ministry for the Third Millennium). Nashville: Abingdon Press, 1999.

"African Americans and Their Faith." A report published by the Barna Research Group.

Brock, Charles. *Indigenous Church Planting: A Practical Journey.* Kansas City, Mo.: Church Growth International, 1990.

Conn, Harvie M., ed. *Planting and Growing Urban Churches: From Dream to Reality.* Grand Rapids, Mich.: Baker Book House, 1997.

Francis, H. E., and Hozell C. Francis. *Church Planting in the African-American Context.* Grand Rapids, Mich.: Zondervan, 1999.

Galloway, Dale, and Kathi Mills. *The Small Group Book: The Practical Guide for Nurturing Christians and Building Churches.* Grand Rapids, Mich.: Fleming H. Revell Co., 1995.

Hesselgrave, David J., and Donald Anderson McGavran. *Planting Churches Cross-Culturally: North America and Beyond.* Grand Rapids, Mich.: Baker Book House, 2000.

Hurn, Raymond W. *The Rising Tide: New Churches for the New Millennium.* Kansas City: Beacon Hill Press, 1997.

Malphurs, Aubrey, et al. *Planting Growing Churches for the 21st Century: A Comprehensive Guide for New Churches and Those Desiring Renewal.* Grand Rapids, Mich.: Baker Book House, 1998.

Mannoia, Kevin W. *Church Planting: The Next Generation.* Indianapolis: Light and Life Communications, 1994.

Shenk, David W., and Ervin R. Stutzman. *Creating Communities of the Kingdom: New Testament Models of Church Planting.* Scottsdale, Pa.: Herald Press, 1988.

Wagner, C. Peter. *Church Planting for a Greater Harvest: A Comprehensive Guide.* Ventura, Calif.: Regal Books, 1990.

ABOUT THE AUTHORS

Rev. Michael J. Cox is director of church planting, National Ministries, American Baptist Churches (ABC) in the U.S.A. Prior to joining the ABC staff in 1998, the Reverend Cox served on the staff of the North American Mission Board of the Southern Baptist Convention. A former church planter and pastor of Faith Community Baptist Church in Euclid, Ohio, Cox received a bachelor of arts degree from Morehouse College in Atlanta, Georgia, and a master of arts degree from Southwestern Baptist Theological Seminary in Fort Worth, Texas.

Dr. Joe Samuel Ratliff has served as pastor of Brentwood Baptist Church in Houston, Texas, since 1980. He has led the congregation to start several churches in diverse parts of the Houston metropolitan area. Dr. Ratliff received a bachelor of

About the Authors

arts degree from Morehouse College in Atlanta, Georgia, and a master of divinity degree and a doctor of ministry degree from the Interdenominational Theological Center in Atlanta, Georgia. He served as assistant professor of religion at Morehouse College from 1975 to 1978 and as visiting professor at Southern Baptist Seminary in Louisville, Kentucky, and at New Orleans Baptist Theological Seminary in Louisiana.